CHECK LIST FOR ENTERTAINING

BARBARA LEE FOLLETT

Dolphin Books
Doubleday & Company, Inc.
Garden City, New York
1976

ISBN: 0-385-04671-5
Library of Congress Catalog Card Number 75-40752
Copyright © 1976 by Barbara Lee Follett
All Rights Reserved
Printed in the United States of America
First Edition

To Ben,
with love and thanks

ACKNOWLEDGMENTS

My grateful thanks to our friend, Mr. Harry Haehl, Honorary Consul General for Malaysia in California, for his advice and help on "Diplomatic and Military Protocol," and to his gracious wife, Helen, for her help.

Jack Daniels, also our friend, was my advisor on "Party Decorating." Mr. Daniels, internationally known lecturer and author, color consultant, and instructor-lecturer in floral design, is instructor in art at College of San Mateo, San Mateo, California.

And my deepest appreciation to the many others who have generously shared their expertise.

CONTENTS

LIST OF RECIPES

CHECK LIST FOR
ENTERTAINING

1. FIRST THOUGHTS

Entertaining is a lovely and important part of life—a pleasure for guests and hosts alike.

When you sincerely enjoy inviting friends to your home, they will inevitably respond to your warmth and hospitality, no matter how simply or elaborately you entertain them. Entertaining is even more fun when you can feel like a guest at your own party.

Feeling like a guest is not as difficult as it might seem. All it requires is proper planning and advance preparation. Without thoughtful planning and preparation, one becomes rushed, confused or harassed, and consequently cannot be a relaxed hostess.

The purpose of this book is to help you plan in a way that will ease your entertaining and make it more enjoyable. A glance at the chapter headings will show that every phase has been considered, and within each chapter you will find reminders and check lists to answer your questions and solve your problems.

My previous book, *Check List for a Perfect Wedding*, was written by request—to fill a need. Friends realized that a successful, serene wedding depends upon the planning that goes beforehand.* Brides and their mothers need the assurance that nothing is left undone; they know it is too late by the wedding day to change plans, remedy mistakes, or add forgotten details.

So it is with *Check List for Entertaining;* it too is written by request—to fill a comparable need. Hostesses also want the assurance that they have remembered everything before it is too late.

Fulfilling the request for this book has been both a

---

* Editor's Note: Now over half a million users of Mrs. Follett's book enthusiastically agree.

pleasure and a revelation. If I were a model housekeeper, gourmet cook and efficiency expert, I doubt if writing this book would have intrigued me. Rather, it is because I am *not* one of those models that the subject sparked my imagination. I am simply a busy person who adds new interest, challenges, and hobbies while never abandoning old ones. The crux of the problem for most of us is finding time for all our interests, plus the entertaining we love to do.

If you are looking for The One Right Way to entertain, this book cannot give you the answer. Any number of ways can be "right" if they suit your own style, capabilities and wishes. Style need not follow a static, in-a-rut pattern, nor be a mirror image of friends' parties. Surprise your guests occasionally with a welcome change of pace— then let them imitate you.

If this is your first venture into entertaining on your own, this book will help you sort out your thoughts and give you ideas toward establishing your own style. Each time you entertain, you will gain confidence and skill to make the next occasion easier.

Experienced hostesses will also find suggestions for managing their time and energy by organizing in advance. The unavailability or expense of extra help calls for logical reasoning and adaptability.

A hostess should not try to duplicate by herself the sort of parties she would customarily give with help (a mistake I have made); nor should she forfeit home entertaining (another mistake I've made). Instead, she can find less demanding ways to entertain and follow the trend toward informality.

We tend to continue doing things the way we've always done them—by habit more than by thought. If we stop to ask ourselves if there is an easier way, we often find both an easier and *better* way. Sometimes we think we are overburdened with work. Seldom does the actual work create the burden; more often it is the concern, worry and indecisions that weigh us down.

I hope this book will encourage you to make your own decisions, and give you the confidence to carry them through with the ease and pleasure that will make you a guest at your own party.

Although this book is directed to "the hostess," it applies to everyone alike. Husbands and single hosts: my thoughts, ideas and best wishes include *you!*

Happy entertaining.

NOTES TO THE HOSTESS

1. Entertaining is yours to carry through as *you* wish. Whether hospitality takes the form of setting an extra place at the table or planning a party, let it reflect *your* ideas.

2. Hospitality is never measured in dollars and cents; don't strain the budget.

3. Guests are always flattered when you entertain them in your home.

4. Introductions: At a dinner or small party, see that all guests are introduced to one another. At a large affair, such as a tea or cocktail party where it is impossible to introduce everyone, watch to see that no one is left alone.

   If you see someone standing alone, draw him into your conversation with a quick briefing, "Won't you join us? We were talking about . . ."

5. In general, avoid pessimistic topics. Remember, it's a party!

6. After you provide all the necessary elements for the party, forget the mechanics and see that your guests enjoy themselves. The guest is king!

7. Be alert to your guests' comforts, but don't flutter and hover over them.

8. Asterisks sprinkled sparsely throughout this book indicate that recipes follow at the end of the chapter.

While this book is not a cookbook, a few recipes were selected as good examples of do-aheads—the hostess' godsend.

9. You will find check lists and suggestions in every chapter—more than you might need at any single affair. Look them over to reassure yourself you have remembered everything. If a reminder does not fit your plan, don't fret over it—forget it.

Again—remember it is *your* party!

Let the ideas in the following chapters serve as springboards for your own ingenuity.

On with the planning . . .

2. WAYS TO INVITE

As soon as you mail or telephone that first invitation the party is launched. But wait! Don't invite until you first think the party through so you can make your intentions clear.

WHOM TO INVITE

1. Head the guest list with your own names. I once neglected to do this and found myself trying to seat twelve at a table carefully set for ten. Never since!

2. Don't hesitate to mix guests. A few strangers will stimulate better conversation.

3. If you are dubious about inviting a guest because of the late dinner hour, or the number of stairs he would have to climb, give him the pleasure of knowing you would like him to come. He knows his own limitations, and can accept or refuse on his own.

4. One needn't invite an equal number of men and women. To quote a friend, "I thought we came to eat, not to mate."

5. When inviting a single woman, arrange to have someone pick her up. Recently a single woman's friends drove across town to pick her up, while her next door neighbors, not knowing she had been invited to the same party, drove alone. The hostess needed to go only one step further to become the *super*hostess.

6. Single men and women sometimes like to bring a date or escort to a party. If you are willing, write "Date" or "Escort" on the invitation.

   For a smaller party, you might inquire if your guest

would like to bring a friend. If so, ask for the friend's name and address, and mail a personal invitation.

7. When one has to limit the number of guests at a large reception, cocktail party or wedding, how much does she dare overinvite? Caterers estimate that one quarter to one third of those invited will not come, and experience shows that even among those who accept, last minute cancellations will occur. However, if the occasion is as special as a fiftieth anniversary, guests will climb out of sickbeds to attend such a wonderful affair. This "one quarter to one third" formula is a useful guideline to inviting.

INVITING BY TELEPHONE

Consider the advantages of inviting by telephone for all but formal or large affairs. An immediate refusal gives time to change the guest list as one goes along, whereas a written refusal could arrive too late to ask another guest.

Just be sure to identify yourself immediately. Telephone-voice mix-ups can bring about strange situations—sometimes amusing, sometimes shattering. I could describe some hair-raising experiences but shall spare you those. Instead, here is an amusing mix-up:

Two men (husbands, that is) relayed their wives' invitation and acceptance via telephone. The caller neglected to mention his name because he assumed the other man recognized his voice.

Outcome: One couple waited with the table set for four, while the other couple went to still another's home, only to find no one there.

"Guess Who's Calling" games are out. They sometimes embarrass and always annoy.

Telephoning gives the hostess a chance to be explicit and to answer questions generally left unsaid in written invitations:

1. What to wear. Guests are uncomfortable if they overdress. The hostess can say, "We're just having another

couple. Tell Bob to wear a sport jacket," or "I am wearing an informal long dress, but wear whatever you like."

If you mean "informal," don't say, "Just casual," except perhaps for a barbecue. The hostess might mean informal summer silk or linen dresses for the ladies, and sport coats for the men while some guests might interpret casual to mean shorts or jeans.

Men want to know if they should wear black tie, suit or sport jacket, so be specific.

"Black tie" means dinner jacket for the men and dinner dress for the ladies, but not necessarily formal. Current women's styles are adaptable; dressy, short dresses, evening pajamas or simple, long dresses are equally suitable for black tie or informal evenings.

2. If your party starts at an intermediate hour such as 8 P.M., do you mean dinner? Dessert? Games? Make your plan clear.

3. Guests are inclined to be more prompt if they know a party will be small. When you phone, you can give a hint—"just a few" . . . "a little dinner" . . . "a party" —or be even more definitive.

We once received a dinner invitation written on an attractive fill-in card. Knowing the hosts' penchant for large, dressy parties and interminable cocktail hours, I dressed accordingly and we arrived somewhat late. To our surprise, the total guest list consisted of ourselves and one other couple.

I had misguessed and was apologetic, but I still wonder why for such a small dinner, the hostess didn't telephone in the first place.

4. If you invite guests for a 12:30 weekend lunch and precede it with a two-hour cocktail period, by the time lunch is served, those who arrived on time will be disgruntled, starved or prone. Specify the time lunch will be served: "Cocktails at 12:30, lunch at 2:00," and

let guests set their own arrival time. For dinners: "Cocktails at 7:15, dinner at 8:30."

5. Barbecue invitations need to be especially specific. We were invited for a "swim and barbecue about 1:30" which sounded like swimming first, to be followed by a midafternoon or late-day barbecue. At two o'clock the host phoned to say he was waiting to broil our steaks. We dashed over, never admitting we had just finished eating hot dogs and an enormous clean-out-the-refrigerator salad.

6. Reminder cards are valuable adjuncts to a telephoned invitation. If you wish to send reminders, mail them about ten days to two weeks before the occasion.

A reminder card is similar to an invitation in that it includes date, time, place, and if black tie. However, at the top of the card, it states "Reminder," or "To Remind," and does not ask for a response.

A quality post card will do; a calling card is even better; but most convenient of all is the slightly larger 3¼ by 4⅝ inches, engraved or processed white or bordered French note.

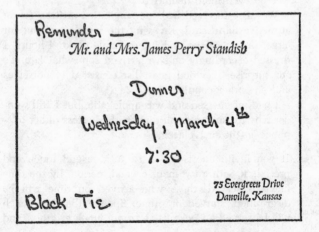

THE WRITTEN INVITATION

The same prior cautioning—be explicit—applies to a written invitation. One may use any form, informal or formal, as long as it is consistent with the style of entertaining.

Stationers carry a wide variety of attractive informal invitations ready to be filled in. They can also advise you about wording and styles of formal invitations if you wish to have them processed, printed or engraved, or they can provide you with the proper unembellished formal stationery for writing your own.

Check List for the Written Invitation:

1. When writing an informal note, remember to add your last name unless it is printed on your stationery.

2. You will find it easy to compose or respond to third-person formal invitations if you will follow a few simple guidelines:

   —Work out the spacing of whatever you wish to say so the center of each phrase touches an imaginary line drawn down the center of the paper, as opposed to paragraph style.

   —Write out the date and time; use no figures except for house numbers and zip code.

   —Write the names in full without using initials.

   —Example:

Mr. and Mrs. James Standish
request the pleasure of your company
at dinner
on Friday, the fourth of March
at half past seven o'clock
The Hillsdale Club

Please Respond
75 Evergreen Drive
Danville, Kansas 10389

The name of the invited guest may be substituted for "your company," and the spacing adjusted accordingly.

—Envelopes should be carefully addressed without abbreviations, except for "Mr." and "Mrs."

3. It is not necessary to say cocktails; guests will assume that a dinner invitation includes a cocktail period. Save the terms, "Cocktails and Dinner" or "Cocktails and Buffet," for the kinds of parties where the emphasis is on a cocktail party (page 87).

4. On a calling card the names are centered. On a French note, which is larger, the names are above center, leaving space for writing an invitation or brief message. The address can be engraved or processed in either the lower-right or upper-right corner.

5. R.S.V.P., R.s.v.p., Rsvp, Please Reply, and Please Respond all say the same thing and are used interchangeably. "The favor of a reply is requested" is the more formal wording.

6. Be sure to include an address or telephone number for responses, especially if the party will not be held in your home. A return address is not enough.

7. Some invitations, instead of requesting responses, use the term, "Regrets only," a sure clue to a large party. I prefer responses as insurance against lost invitations.

8. As much as I love using my smooth, nylon-tipped pen, I should put it aside when addressing conventional engraved wedding or other formal invitations unless it has a fine point. Black ink is best; blue-black next best; colored ink out.

9. When giving a large party, make an alphabetical master list using only last names.

Tape your list in a convenient place to check responses. Note the *number* of people who accept—for example, Anderson 1, Andrews 2. This will make it easy to arrive at the final total. Cross off the names of people who send regrets.

10. If you want to carry out a special theme, create your own original invitations. They will reflect the spirit of the party.

   We had fun with a shipwreck-party invitation. We charred the edges of our handwritten invitations and inserted them into small bottles which we sent in mailing tubes.

11. Cocktail party invitations are discussed fully starting on page 85.

ABOUT RESPONSES

Even without an Rsvp, every invitation should be acknowledged.

When giving a dinner, one must have an accurate count. If someone has not answered by a reasonable length of time, the hostess may telephone to find out "if the invitation went astray." If friends delay answering Open House invitations, the hosts must fall back on the "one quarter to one third won't come" formula (page 6).

FRIENDS' HOUSEGUESTS

Hosts often wonder if they must include their friends' visitors. While not mandatory, it is gracious and helpful if they can manage it.

Friends should not *ask* to bring houseguests; instead they should explain that they must decline or cancel because of visitors. That leaves the option up to the hostess, either to include the extra guests or to say she is sorry she cannot invite the visitors at that time. Perhaps she can do something else for them and give the friends a rain check to another dinner.

From the other viewpoint, having been houseguests, I understand a certain reluctance when one is invited only because of his friends.

As we tagged along one evening to a large black tie dinner, we wondered if we were imposing—if the hostess might have been cornered into including us.

Our doubts were dispelled in less than ten seconds by the supreme warmth as the hosts welcomed and thanked us for coming. Place cards indicated that we were the guests of honor that evening—seated to the right of the host and hostess.

Although this generous gesture was a compliment to the friends who brought us, it was also an indication of the ideal hosts' empathy and graciousness.

ONE MORE PAUSE

Will you need extra help for this party? Then "inviting" the help has top priority before inviting the guests.

I recall a hostess' impromptu invitation. "The van der Hacks are coming Friday, and I'm trying to get a quick dinner party together." We were delighted to accept because we always enjoyed this particular couple's out-of-town friends.

At the party when I saw no unfamiliar faces, I asked the hostess where her houseguests were.

"What houseguests?" she asked.

"The guests of honor—the couple the party's for," I explained. She still looked baffled, so I continued, "The van something or others—"

She burst out laughing, then pointed to the man serving drinks and the waitress passing hors d'oeuvres, the van der Hacks—first "invited," most important.

3. ADVANCE ORGANIZING

Jot it down, then take care of everything *bit by bit*. Those words are the key to the non-frazzled hostess, and a necessity to those who work or are otherwise occupied during the daytime.

Idea flashes are too transitory to risk losing. Jot them down whenever they come—on a pad by your bedside or in the car, on the bathroom mirror with a felt-tipped pen, on the steamy shower door to transfer quickly before it fades. Notes for this book were originally written in all those unlikely places. If any of the ideas seem hazy, maybe they were the steamy ones.

There are those rare people who have the physical and emotional make-up to leave everything until the last minute, and still enjoy the party. If you are like that, bravo! But, if you are like most of us, you have learned to expect the unexpected—the sink clogs, the dog wanders away, or your youngster forgets to tell you he needs four dozen cookies that day for the school bake sale.

Lists can be lifesavers—write out tomorrow's agenda today. You won't accomplish everything on it, but the list will get you off to a good start. Do the hardest or most distasteful job first; everything else will seem easy by comparison.

Save yourself the unnecessary, last-minute, exhausting push and flurry by using from the following check lists whatever suits your life style, temperament and type of entertaining.

This detailed procedure applies only to your most ambitious parties, not every time you spontaneously entertain an extra couple.

DAYS OR WEEKS AHEAD

By now you have invited your guests and have your general plan in mind—whether buffet or sit-down, alone or with help. Now you can work on the specifics:

1. Plan your menu and post it on the refrigerator door or a bulletin board. Take into consideration your equipment and who will cook. With one oven, be careful not to plan foods which require different temperatures.

2. At your convenience, make up the shopping list. Try breaking your list into three parts:

   —Advance ordering and buying: staples, canned goods, freezables, candles, paper goods and other household needs.

   —A day or two before: perishables—meat or poultry and flowers.

   —The party day: no more than picking up fresh sea food or ice, unless your freezer holds enough.

3. Gradually cook and freeze when you have time. Many desserts and hors d'oeuvres freeze well.

4. If you telephoned the invitations, send reminder cards, if you wish, ten days to two weeks ahead of the party.

5. Look over your linens.

6. Arrange table seating (page 28) and make place cards or a chart in BIG letters.

7. Decide what to wear and fix the hook that always irritates your husband. Are his clothes ready?

   Learn a lesson from a friend who dieted madly before her party. She forgot that while *she* was shrinking, her dress was *not*. Crisis just before the party!

TWO OR MORE DAYS BEFORE THE PARTY

The following list should be staggered over several days or evenings, or *you* will be staggering.

1. Round up extra tables or other equipment as early as the lender can spare them.

2. Polish flat silver. If silver serving dishes were stored airtight in plastic wrap, they are ready to use.

3. Do essential cleaning. Note the word, "essential,"—not ready for white-glove inspection.

4. Family life can't be put out in limbo while you concentrate on preparations, so plan ahead for leftovers the preparty evening.

5. Set the dining table a day or so ahead for a party, and picnic on trays or TV tables someplace else.

   —If you have someone to help, she will know how to set *a* table but not *your* table.

   —Use only the flat silver your menu requires.

   —Set out serving dishes and the accompanying servers.
   For buffets: Set platters on the buffet table as a double check that you have everything you need. In each serving dish, place a slip of paper noting what goes into it. The notes will jar your memory and guarantee no charred rolls in the oven the next morning.

6. Set out dessert dishes and complete coffee service.

7. If you plan to use greenery in flower arrangements, pick and clean it and soak in deep water. Prepare containers.

8. Unless your home is always a model of neatness, begin uncluttering it. Carry a tray or basket to gather misplaced items and distribute them as you move about the house.

9. Check coasters, ash trays, cigarette boxes and matches.

THE DAY BEFORE THE PARTY

Make this your *do-everything* day, so you can loaf on the party day. Those who are not home during the daytime can change the timetable to take care of several of these tasks in the preceding evenings.

1. Recheck your list and finish marketing; by now you should have little left to buy.

2. Buy flowers or pick them in the morning; harden them according to their individual needs (page 149); arrange later in the day.

3. Then attack kitchen preparations. Many sauces improve when flavors have time to blend; taste them the next day, and add more seasoning if needed.

4. Mark the time to start cooking each dish on your menu.

5. Is it time for a tension-breaker? After ten minutes you will be refreshed, and ready for the next set of tasks (page 207, item 23).

6. Put cold drinks to chill. Will you or your husband take care of the wine? Does he need reminding?

7. Is the fire set, and extra logs close at hand?

8. Dust the house and swoop the clutter from your desk into a drawer—don't forget which drawer.

9. This was a full day. Now take time to fix your nails and hair.

THE PARTY DAY

This day should be fun now that tasks are at a minimum.

1. Flip the dustcloth over table tops—or blow!

2. Check to see if flowers need a drink of water.

3. After the last shower, put out your prettiest bath and guest towels.

4. Dress early. The more I rush to dress the longer it takes me because I inevitably smear my mascara or drop a contact lens.

5. A burned-down fire is prettier and less crackly than a newly lighted one. Light it early, and give yourself leeway in case it smokes.

6. One last check in the kitchen to see that you are following your cooking time chart.

The transformation from cook to hostess entails more than removing your kitchen apron. Mentally go out the back door and enter the front door. Curtain! New scene! Enter the hostess-guest at your own party!

4. YOUR MEMORY BANK

I couldn't live without my hostess file; at least I couldn't live *as well!* My records have paid dividends over and over again, as they became blueprints for subsequent entertaining.

My first records were sketchy, but I soon discovered they had to be detailed and complete to be of real value. When I referred to them later, they reminded me of everything to do and, equally important, of everything *not* to do again.

It doesn't matter how you keep your records as long as they are clear to you. Devise your own charts or card-file system, or use a loose-leaf binder or printed hostess book.

WHAT TO RECORD, AND WHY

1. *Basic but necessary:*

   —Date and time.

   —Total number of guests.

   —Names of guests so you can avoid the same combinations, especially at small dinners.

   —Detailed menu, including a notation where to find recipes—cookbooks used and page numbers of recipes.

   —Caterer's, or other help's, name.

2. *Detailed but important:*

   —Shopping list down to the last olive. What a boon if you decide to repeat that particular menu. Record prices, too, if you wish.

—Arranging tables. Once you've figured out how best to arrange extra tables, keep the plan. Also note unusual decorations you liked well enough to do again.

—To-borrow list: card tables, folding chairs, extra silverware, and a large coffee maker.

—Reminders, such as ice, mixes, and cocktail napkins.

3. *After-the-party secrets for your eyes only:*
   The next day while impressions are vivid, take a few minutes to write frank, pertinent notes, such as:

—"Forget yogurt dip. N.G."

—"Betty always late. Count on it."

—"Bill says he loves Mexican food. Make enchiladas."

—"Chicken recipe fabulous. Do again."

—"Light fire earlier. One hour ahead." (If you've barbecued.)

—"For curry dinner, use bleachable napkins," tells the story of your entire morning working with stain remover.

—For this party, you probably had to guess what quantities to buy. Next to your shopping list, note amounts to buy in the future. It will be easy to adjust up or down proportionately for a different number.

Why would one bother to write all these details? Because after the thinking and planning are completed, that same meal could be repeated in half the time—*with improvements.*

Don't misunderstand. I do not advocate confining your entire cooking repertoire to one good menu for each type of entertaining, in spite of a friend's half-joking observation. She said, "It is easier to find a new set of friends than another foolproof menu!"

I hope these examples have persuaded you to start keeping records. As you fill out the first page or card, you might think it a waste of time, but as your records build up over the months and years, you will find them as useful as an extra brain.

5. WAYS TO SERVE EASILY AND CORRECTLY

If a hostess can make her work look effortless, that is the biggest favor she can do for her guests, because only then can they relax. Looking effortless is just a matter of serving quietly, with the fewest interruptions and trips to the kitchen.

Easy to serve buffets and semibuffets are discussed in the following chapter. This section is confined to various options for serving a three-course, informal, sit-down dinner.

First-course Options

1. Serve soup—hot in winter, chilled in summer—in the living room. See page 32 for other first-course suggestions to serve in the living room.

    While guests finish their first course you will have a few moments to light candles, pour water, and get the main course ready. Important: Double check the refrigerator so the cranberry sauce slated for tonight's dinner won't remain there to greet you in the morning.

2. Instead of a first course in the living room, you can consolidate first and second courses by placing salads to the left and eating them along with the main course.

3. Do you prefer the traditional three separate courses at the table? If so, before you announce dinner, set the first course at each place on a service plate or dinnersize plate.

    As you see, this third option entails clearing the table one extra time.

Main-course Serving Choices

1. The host or hostess serves at the table, or from a cart or card table alongside, "family style." Passing one plate to the right, the next to the left, tends to stop them from circling the table.

2. Place the dinner on a buffet where there is more room to carve and serve. Guests remain seated and hosts bring the plates to them.

3. Serve the plates individually in the kitchen. Think color to make them attractive (page 146). If you wish, one guest may help carry them to the table, but by all means avoid the chaos of letting all the ladies jump up at one time.

Wine

The host pours the wine. For eight people, place another bottle or decanter at the other end of the table and ask one of the men to take care of the four guests nearest him. A hostess who is alone often asks one of the men to take over wine pouring, mainly because she has other things to do.

Clearing the Table Before Dessert

Take the dishes directly to the kitchen, or place them all on a cart and wheel it out. Scan the table and remove everything not needed at dessert time—salts and peppers, unused silver, condiments, sauce and bread. Leave beverage glasses on the table.

Dessert Serving Options

Earlier in the day, set up a tray or cart with everything you will need for dessert and coffee and serve it any of the following ways:

1. Bring dessert and a stack of plates for the host or hostess to serve at the table.

2. Bring individual desserts directly from the kitchen to the guests.

3. Place empty dessert plates in front of the guests. Pass dessert and let them serve themselves.

4. Do not place dessert silver alongside other silverware. Bring it in at dessert time (correct for either informal or formal service), or place it crossways at the upper edge of the place setting (correct for informal service only).

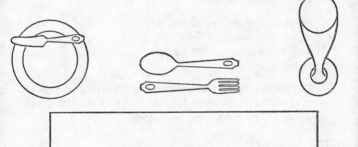

5. Serve coffee with dessert if you like to linger at the table, or take it into the living room on a tray.

SERVING WITH HELP

Ideally, serving procedures are identical for both informal and formal meals, and are used daily in some homes with experienced help. For detailed descriptions of this type of service, turn to page 40.

First consider those guidelines, then feel free to adapt them to your help's ability, the number to be served, or simply your preference. Asking one maid to serve a three-course, sit-down dinner to eight persons will surely call for some short cuts, especially if she also has kitchen responsibilities. Only the variations, short cuts and options will be discussed in this chapter.

First-course Serving Variations

1. Place the first course on the table before announcing dinner. In this case, napkins will be placed to the left of the forks. If you haven't service plates—also referred to as place plates—substitute dinner-sized plates. They are only slightly smaller and will serve the purpose.

2. If you prefer, ask the maid to bring in servings for two people at one time.

3. Another alternative: Serve soup in the living room. When you come to the table, have a service plate at each place and you are ready to proceed with the next course.

4. Place crackers on the butter plate or first-course plate to give the maid more time in the kitchen. Eliminate butter plates if rolls are prebuttered.

Clearing First-course Dishes

Usually the maid exchanges a dinner plate for the service plate and first course at one time.

Exception: The maid leaves the service plate and removes only the first-course dish if she is later to bring plates served individually from the kitchen.

The fine line of distinction between the two procedures —leaving or removing service plates—follows the premise that a plate with food on it should be exchanged only for an empty plate.

Main-course Serving Variations

1. The host carves with the maid stationed at his side. As he serves each plate, she takes it to exchange for a guest's plate, which she then takes back to the host.

2. The host has a stack of plates at hand. As he serves each plate, he passes it to a guest, who in turn passes it

on. This more expedient and informal option frees the maid to start passing vegetables and rolls, or to refill water glasses.

3. The maid either passes sauces, relishes and condiments or places them alongside the hostess to start around the table.

4. Each plate may be individually served directly from the kitchen.

5. Experienced help will watch and know when to pass second servings. If help is not experienced, the hostess can ring and signal by a gesture, or quietly tell what is needed.

    The platter should be reorganized so it is as attractive as the first time. It will be more tempting if larger slices of meat or pieces of chicken are cut in half.

6. Before dessert, the maid clears the table completely of everything that will not be needed. Without stacking dishes, she may take whatever she can carry in two hands.

Dessert Serving Options

1. The maid may bring individual dessert to each place.

2. Dessert and a stack of plates may be placed in front of the host or hostess to serve.

    —The maid stations herself alongside and takes a serving to each guest.

    —Or, while the maid brings in coffee, the hostess may hand dessert to the next guest to pass along.

Finger Bowls?

A finger bowl is a necessity after eating cracked crab or lobster. Proper placement is to the left side above the forks, on a plate with a doily.

At dessert time, finger bowls are optional at an informal dinner. If you wish to use them, refer to page 42, item 10.

Serving Coffee

There is no right or wrong way to serve coffee at an informal dinner. Some people enjoy it at the table with dessert, in which case the men are often given large cups, the ladies small, or each may be asked his preference. Others find it pleasant to bring a coffee tray with demitasses into the living room, where either the hostess or a maid may pour it.

More than Six or Eight

A sit-down dinner for ten, twelve or more, with the type of service outlined in this section, requires an extra person to serve. If it is impractical to engage more help, change to buffet service (page 33).

A Questioned Variation

One rule of etiquette states that the lady guest of honor must be served first. Some knowledgeable hostesses, even while aware of the rule, prefer being served first at *informal* dinners. Why?

—The hostess prefers to check what comes from the kitchen to instantly correct an omission, or change an unwieldy serving implement before others are served.

—The hostess would rather struggle to extricate a difficult first serving, and leave easier servings for her guests.

—She can set an example when she adds a sauce to the meat instead of the vegetables, or when she shows how to attack a mysterious-looking dish.

—When the hostess takes a second serving—even a token one—others, who might have been reluctant, are more apt to follow her lead.

The question has been asked and reasons explained, but the decision remains up to each hostess personally. Undoubtedly the experience of her help will be a factor.

There is no doubt about it. A hostess is more relaxed with a maid to serve at a dinner party; however, this is not always practical. When serving is the hostess' responsibility, here is one more reminder: Never try to pinch-hit for a maid. Instead, clear one course completely, and use one of the options outlined in the earlier part of this chapter. You will do beautifully.

6. DINNERS

A glance at the chapter headings will remind you of the many different ways to entertain. Each way can be special, and in time you will probably try them all. However, because most women work, or are involved during the day with families or outside activities, they entertain more frequently at dinners.

If you plan to spend time on any one chapter, I suggest you spend it here because dinner-party logistics apply to other entertaining. For example, buffets which are outlined here work perfectly for lunches, barbecues and other parties discussed later in the book. This detailed chapter is placed early so you can transfer its ideas to other entertaining.

Occasionally you will find a reference to "simple" entertaining which is not meant to be derogatory. Remember, simplicity carries its own elegance.

SEATING

Instead of having to make flash decisions while guests stand and wait, it is easier if the hostess plans her seating arrangement ahead of time.

If the party is small, she indicates where guests are to sit. For more than eight, place cards written in LARGE letters are convenient. When two or more tables are used, a seating chart can be placed on an easel or taped to the wall.

How to seat guests of honor is discussed in the chapter on Protocol, page 181; however, additional diagrams might be useful.

The first two diagrams below are self-explanatory. The third is our complete scramble to avoid honoring one couple more than another. Mrs. A. and Mrs. B. are seated

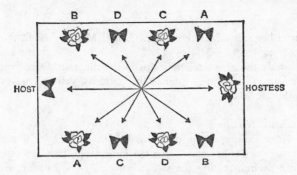

Honoring One Couple

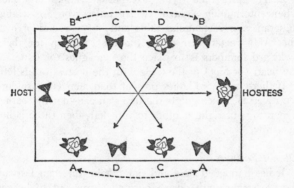

Honoring Two Couples

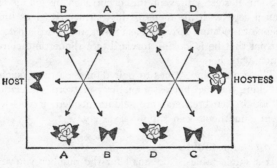

Each Couple Honored

on either side of the host, Mr. C. and Mr. D. beside the hostess.

Study the arrow relationships in the diagram. Once you understand and can visualize the patterns, you will never feel at a loss.

Difficult Numbers

After looking at the diagrams you might wonder if our dinner parties are always for ten guests. No, they are not, even though seating ten works out easily—as do four, six or fourteen.

Don't waste time trying to alternate ladies and men when entertaining eight or twelve unless you are willing to scrap your rectangular table and buy a round or oval one. At a rectangular table, the best solution for these awkward numbers is to place the man guest of honor at the head (or foot) of the table with the hostess to his left.

If there are more ladies present than men (it is seldom the reverse), space guests the best you can—not by seating a man to your right, another to your left, then three ladies in a row.

Dinner Partners

It has happened time and time again—the man I spend the most time with during cocktails turns out to be my dinner partner.

Some hostesses prevent this occurrence by giving each man a card with the name of his partner. It gives him a chance to locate a lady he hasn't met, or to explain to his partner that he is looking forward to a dinnertime conversation with her.

There are many games to pair dinner partners, such as matching the two halves of pictures or word associations. Although "ice breakers" are seldom needed, if you want them game books can supply a variety.

Two or More Tables

If a single table is too small for the number you've invited, work it out as evenly as you can.

For twelve: four—four—four at card tables, or six—six at the dining table and two card tables placed end to end.

For ten: six—four, or five—five.

At a larger buffet party of sixteen or more, the hosts sometimes leave seating to chance, knowing that any grouping will prove enjoyable.

Table Charts

At a large party, a chart in addition to place cards will help guests find their places easily. Post it in a conspicuous place.

1. Try for larger than normal printing or writing. Idea: Typewriters for the visually handicapped are made with oversized print. If you can locate one—possibly through a volunteer bureau or Braille center—you might be given permission to use it, especially if you make a contribution. Typewriters used in primary grades also have large type. Check with a nearby elementary school to see if such a typewriter is available.

2. Arranging names alphabetically makes them easy to find, but does nothing toward identifying table mates.

3. Groupings by table number are better. A man can take one of the ladies at his table in to dinner unless he sees that his wife has been left stranded. Then he can take her to her table, as well.

4. One can use a different-colored cloth at each table, then paint the same colored rectangles on the chart. The names on the various colors make child's play of finding one's table.

5. There can be, and often are, last-day disappointments, too late to rearrange seating and make a new chart. Guests will understand if their table is unbalanced. Have the extra place settings and chairs removed.

A FOURSOME

It makes no difference whether we are hosts or guests at foursome dinners, we consider them special. As guests, we feel extremely complimented when an evening is planned for us alone. Our own guests seem to react with the same enthusiasm to these friendly, comfortable evenings.

An elegant dinner is seldom the object of a foursome evening, while good companionship is. We've had some delightful foursome evenings when we've eaten hamburgers, sent out for a Chinese dish, or pooled our dinners on the spur of the moment.

When we entertain I don't want to spend one unnecessary moment away from our guests. I have finally settled on a formula for a simple menu, and a way of serving that takes me away from the table only once.

1. First course in the living room or patio.

If all four enjoy a game, it is pleasant to play and nibble during the predinner period.

Warning: Depend on a timer to keep your logistics straight—when to put dinner in the oven, take it out, or start a barbecue fire. Definitely more dependable than clock-watching.

Whether drinks consist of juice, wine or cocktails, appetizers are planned as an integral part of dinner— not a supplement. Leave the appetite-spoilers such as bready canapés, nuts or chips for cocktail parties.

At first glance, the following list might appear lavish, but remember, what you serve can take the place of one or two courses—the equivalent of salad and soup, salad and sea food or sea food and soup. Try one or two varieties from the following four classifications:

—Salad substitute. Crisp, chilled, raw vegetables, including young, uncooked, sliced mushrooms, with curried or other seasoned dip.

—Sea food, such as prawns, or caviar mousse.*

—Something hot, often incorporating cheese,* baked before guests arrive and kept hot in a chafing dish or on a hot tray.

—Soup one can drink from a cup or mug (page 62). While guests finish their soup, put your main course on a buffet or side table and let them help themselves on the way to the dinner table.

2. This formula calls for a ready-to-bake main course.

A meat, fish or chicken casserole* which includes both starch and vegetable is ideal. Next best is baking the vegetable at the same time (page 157). Add rolls and condiments if you wish.

If you want to eliminate cooking entirely, plan a beef fondue Bourguignonne. The name is confusing. It is called beef fondue Bourguig*nonne,* while the glorified stew is called Bourguig*non.* All you need besides your fondue equipment and hot oil, placed within easy reach of all, are cubes of choice beef and a few spicy dipping sauces (consult a fondue cookbook).

3. Dessert is simple.* Linger at the table with coffee or serve it in the living room.

This serving-solver formula is as satisfactory for six or eight as for four.

BUFFET DINNER OR SUPPER

Buffet service is popular, and adaptable to any number from four guests to hundreds. A buffet can range in style from simplicity to elegance, from casual dress to black tie, from do-it-yourself to well-staffed affairs. Guests can sit on the floor or at preset tables. Anything goes, as long as it is consistent throughout.

Buffet suppers which sometimes follow cocktail parties are discussed in chapter 12.

Various Ways of Handling Buffet Dinners:

1. Set places at tables, complete with silver, linens, and glassware, with or without place cards.

   The first course is dispensed with, or soup may be served in the living room.

2. Instead of tables with set places, guests may sit in small groups wherever they want. They pick up silver and napkins from the buffet table where it is arranged in an attractive pattern.

3. If you provide enough small tables, you may serve meat that needs cutting, otherwise, choose fork food, such as veal scallopini, curry, or any of the hundreds of ground meat, sea food or boned chicken combinations.

4. Individual lap trays are convenient. Arrange each tray as a place setting with a mat, napkin, silver, and beverage, be it water, wine or coffee. For lap balancing, fork food is advisable.

5. Kitchen buffet.

   Some kitchens are beautifully equipped and more glamorous than many living rooms. They sometimes incorporate a family room or other comfortable seating area. A breakfast bar can serve as a convenient buffet, ready to hold dishes taken directly from the oven, stove, refrigerator or barbecue.

   If yours is the glamorous kitchen, start collecting decorative double-duty utensils for cooking and serving.

6. A Sunday buffet is often an informal supper.
   Suggestions:

   —spaghetti or cannelloni, French bread, salad, red wine

   —crêpes (ham, chicken, mushroom)

   —cold poached fish

   —cold roasted meats or turkey, salads

—casseroles

—chafing dish specials such as rarebit or fondue, with cubed French bread and lots of raw vegetables for salad and dipping.

More Thoughts About Buffet Dinners

1. Keep in mind when planning your buffet menu that everything will be served on one plate. Avoid sauces and dressings that will intermingle.

2. Spiced peaches, pickled beets, kumquats, watermelon pickles or other condiments add a dash of color and beauty to your table and dinner plates.

3. Do a trial run of serving dishes and platters on your buffet table to be certain you have the right sizes and that they look well together (page 15).

4. When placing platters and bowls of food on the buffet table, arrange them in logical sequence so that guests won't have to backtrack. Place rice ahead of curry or creamed dishes, and each sauce, dressing or condiment next to the dish it relates to. Leave space enough between serving dishes to put down a plate so guests will have two free hands.

I am convinced a buffet is the smoothest, most convenient way to serve with a minimum of help or alone.

INFORMAL

An informal dinner refers to one of several kinds of sit-down service, already covered in detail starting on page 21. Unlike a buffet, guests remain seated throughout dinner, and are served by the hosts or a maid.

Informal table appointments may be colorful or not, mats may be used instead of a tablecloth, and dessert silver may be placed at upper edge of mat (page 23).

The words "casual" and "informal" are sometimes mistakenly used interchangeably.

Casual is defined as "unpremeditated . . . offhand . . . leaving to chance . . ." None of these definitions can apply to even the most informal dinner to which one invites guests. Informal means "unceremonious . . . unassuming . . ." No matter how unceremonious a dinner might be, it requires a thought-out plan.

Conceivably, a casual dinner could take place if friends drop in unexpectedly and you ask them to stay. Together you search the Mother Hubbard refrigerator which, by chance, reveals little more than eggs. Ah! Omelettes! That can be fun, too, and is unpremeditated and *casual*.

SEMIBUFFET

A semibuffet is a compromise between an informal sit-down dinner and a buffet.

1. Set the dining room table, or card tables, for a sit-down dinner.

2. The first course is placed at the table before announcing dinner.

3. After the first course, guests serve themselves the main course from the buffet table.

4. If there are several tables, there is less confusion if guests serve themselves table by table. Try to handle this procedure with a light, easy manner—not like a grade school row-by-row fire drill.

5. The hosts or a maid can help serve at the buffet table.

6. As hostess, you leave the buffet table last. Cover serving dishes to keep food hot for second servings. Use precut foil tops if dishes do not have their own lids.

7. Dessert may be served:

—At the dinner table.

—From the buffet table where the guests may again serve themselves. Without help, this method entails the extra work and confusion of clearing both tables, then resetting the buffet.

—In the living room with coffee. This means, get up and walk away from it all. Forget the dishes. Forget everything.

Suggestions for desserts in the living room:

—Ice cream and sauce, served in glass mugs with handles.

—Small cookies or tiny petit fours. No plates will be needed.

—On a winter night if your group is small enough to permit a bit of ceremony and staging in front of a fire, set a chafing dish where your guests can watch your act with a flambé dessert (page 99).

BUSINESS ENTERTAINING

The boss and his wife are coming to dinner. How wonderful! No, that was not a slip of the typewriter. How wonderful that your husband is proud of you and wants to bring them home!

Your ego should soar leaving no room for a moment of uncertainty—even though you know that traditionally the young wife is *supposed* to have a few qualms.

Just the fact that you are entertaining the boss and his wife at home, rather than in a restaurant, portends "good vibes." They can't help feeling complimented that you didn't take the easy way out.

A few suggestions for business entertaining at home:

1. Concentrate on your guests' pleasure and don't be concerned about your self-image. Do it graciously; there is no better image.

2. Select a dinner menu you are comfortable with.

3. Stay with a traditional dinner the first time.

4. If you have ideas on business matters, keep them a secret.

5. Let first-namesmanship come about naturally, at the right time.

Someday another young business wife will invite you and your husband to dinner. Then you will remember how your confidence grew after that first amiable evening.

A PROGRESSIVE DINNER

A progressive dinner—a separate course at each home—is fun for hosts and guests.

Divide dinner into three parts something like this:

1. Drinks and fairly substantial hors d'oeuvres.

2. Soup and main course, or main course and salad.

3. Dessert, coffee, liqueurs and dancing or games.

Although each hostess might have her specialty, all three should work out the entire menu together for balance and complementary flavors. Left to select individually, the menu could start with fruit cocktail and end with fruit compote. Or worse—a curried dip, chicken curry soup, lamb curry and hot curried fruit. Horrors!

It always takes longer to move from home to home than one estimates, so keep the timetable flexible. The main-course hostess should choose a dish that holds well—not, for instance, rare roast beef. The dessert hostess can save her hot chocolate soufflé for another evening when she can time it accurately.

Three couples to share preparations means easier entertaining for larger numbers. But we experienced a novel progressive dinner for one couple—us alone!

Each of three couples wanted to entertain us during our one-day visit to their city. They finally settled their discussion as to which couple would give the dinner by all three sharing the leisurely evening.

Their brilliant solution gave us the opportunity to see each couple's home, hobbies, collections, children and pets. My husband and I were treated like VIPs at a marvelous evening for eight—three sets of hosts and us.

THE FORMAL DINNER

Much of this book is oriented toward informality; however, this Check List would not be complete without the details of a formal dinner.

Formal does not mean stiff, but it calls for a defined routine of service. No short cuts; no improvising. It is better not to attempt a formal dinner without the proper appointments and an experienced staff. While it might be possible to teach an inexperienced person, proper service takes practice and cannot be accomplished overnight.

Following are distinguishing features of a formal dinner: (References to a maid apply equally to a butler.)

1. A tablecloth is appropriate; individual place mats will not suffice. Napkins, not less than twenty-four inches square, are folded flat and placed on service plates.

2. Butter plates are not used. If rolls are served, they are prebuttered.

3. The table is meticulously set with flat silver arranged in order, by courses, so a guest can use the outside implement first and progress toward the one closest to his plate.

   Exclude dessert silver. It is brought in on the dessert plate (page 42, item 10).

4. Pepper mills are not considered suitable for formal dinners. Twin sets of salt dishes with tiny spoons—one for salt, one for coarse-ground pepper—are a solution.

5. More than three courses are served—probably four or five—with salad preceding dessert, not as a first course.

6. An appropriate wine is served with each course (page 200, item 3). All the glasses to be used are placed near the water goblets. Before serving a new course and pouring a different kind of wine, the finished wine glass is removed from the right—so as not to reach across a guest.

7. For information about smoking at the table at formal dinners, see page 183.

8. When dinner is announced, the host and lady guest of honor lead the way. Each gentleman is previously given a card with his dinner partner's name, or told whom to escort to the table. The hostess and man guest of honor follow last.

Formal Serving
1. Service calls for a procedure of exchanging one plate for another so the place in front of a guest is never clear until just before dessert. The maid removes the used plate with her right hand and immediately replaces it with another plate or course, which she holds in the left hand with a small folded napkin.

2. Everything is served from the left, and may be removed from either the left (smoother) or right, as long as the same pattern is carried out consistently at every place.

3. All serving starts with the lady guest of honor and proceeds in order around the table, ending with the host.

4. *First Courses:*
   After everyone is seated, the maid brings the first course, one at a time, and places it on the service plate.

5. The service plate remains until the fish or main course; only the plates on it are exchanged.

6. *The Main Course:*

   Now the service plate and whatever is on it are removed together, and replaced by a warmed dinner plate.

7. Meat is carved and arranged on platters in the kitchen and presented to each guest to serve himself.

   Warning: Not too large or heavy a platter, especially if the chair backs are high.

   —Two implements, a serving spoon and serving fork, rest on the platter with their handles toward the guest. The guest will replace the implements, but the maid uses her right hand to reposition them securely for the next person's convenience.

   —A platter may be arranged to hold more than one item—for example, slices of meat in the center flanked by small potatoes at one end and vegetables or mushrooms at the other. If the platter contains only the meat, the maid repeats the round with vegetables. Sectioned dishes speed service.

   —If a sauce accompanies a dish, such as hollandaise for asparagus, serve it at the same time, if possible.

   —If twelve or more are at the table, both sides can be served simultaneously from duplicate platters.

8. If salad is to follow the main course, another immediate exchange of plates takes place.

9. *Clearing the Table Before Dessert:*

   —For the first time since coming to the table, the places will be completely cleared. Only the water goblet and dessert wine glass remain.

   —The maid returns from the kitchen with a small tray on which she places salts and peppers. She should also replace used ash trays with fresh ones.

—She returns once again and, using a folded napkin, brushes any crumbs onto a small tray or plate
—usually more a gesture than a necessity.

10. *Dessert and Finger Bowls:*

The maid brings the dessert plate topped by a doily
and finger bowl, not more than a third or half filled
with tepid water. In it one may float a blossom or or-
nament, such as a glass bubble. A dessert fork is on
the plate to the left of the bowl and a dessert spoon to
the right.

The guest removes the fork and spoon from the
plate and places them alongside—still in their same
left- and right-hand positions. Next he picks up the
finger bowl in his right hand, the edge of the doily in
his left, and glides them together, as one, to the left
and above the tip of his dessert fork. The hostess
should attend to hers promptly to set the example.

When the maid is passing dessert, if she sees that a
guest might not have noticed the finger bowl in front
of him, she may start to assist—before he drowns his
éclair in a watery grave.

11. *Serving Coffee:*

Most formal is the custom of ladies going to the living room or sitting room for coffee and liqueurs. The
men stand when the ladies leave, then move to the
host's end of the table for their coffee and liqueurs.

The maid will immediately remove dessert plates,
wine glasses and napkins. She may pour liqueurs, but
more often will place a tray of bottles and glasses before the host.

Formal dinners are gracious, memorable affairs, but remember, they exclude short cuts and improvising. Don't
let that keep you from delving into this chapter to remind
you about the fine points. It is a fact of life that one does
not notice the machinery when things run smoothly. This
chapter provides that machinery.

CO-OPERATIVE PARTIES

The objective is sociability, and nobody cares who gives the party—so let everyone give it together, or at least contribute a part of it.

These parties might take place within a group of close friends who want to meet often, without the expense of a party. Other times the party is for friends who seldom exchange invitations. Perhaps, as members of the same working organization, they decide it is party time. Again a no-host party is the answer.

Many possibilities and variations are open to friends with similar attitudes toward co-operative parties:

1. Box-lunch parties divide the work more equitably than any other kind. Each lady brings enough for two, and shares it with a partner.

2. Co-operative Buffet. Someone—usually the so-called hostess—co-ordinates what each is to bring.

   Hosts can provide as little or as much as they like as long as they make their intentions clear before committing the guest.

3. Some groups think it is easier to order from the "deli" and all chip in, however most hosts would object to collecting money for food served in their homes.

4. Bring Your Own Bottle. Drinks can become the most expensive single item of a party, which is the reason BYOB parties have their place at times, especially among young friends.

   When you invite guests to a BYOB party, invite only those who entertain in the same manner.

THE UNEXPECTEDS

"Stay for dinner" or "Come for dinner." How often are we prepared to say those words on a moment's notice?

There are those provident individuals who always double or triple recipes and freeze extra dinners. In addition, their freezers contain vast amounts of meat and poultry. They are always ready for those unexpected situations.

But what about those of us who haven't freezers, or use our limited available space as a grocery store annex to save trips to the market. We have to depend upon our life-saver emergency shelf. Resolve to stock it now, either with a general assortment or on the basis of a favorite quick recipe to fall back on.

If stocking a general assortment, include the following:

—Soups to serve straight from the can, to combine with other varieties (page 62), or to use as the binder for casseroles.

Store a can or two of consommé in the refrigerator, ever ready for a family or company first course. Add a dab of caviar, a slice of lemon or sour cream; you couldn't do better if you planned for a month.

—Celery hearts. Add grated hard-boiled eggs and top with anchovies for celery Victor salad, or braise for a delicious and different hot vegetable.

—Canned chicken, shrimp or crab, minced clams, perhaps canned ham, and you are ready to entertain royalty or the neighborhood children.

A casserole can travel in any direction or to any country, depending upon seasonings and combinations.

—A See-America-First version, which appeals to adults and children, includes chicken, cream soup, mushrooms, peas and rice or noodles.

—Edge to the exotic Mexican version by using chopped pimientos, chili powder, green chilies, black olives and crushed tortilla chips.

—Go oriental with crab or chicken, soy sauce, thin-sliced celery and water chestnuts, layered alternately with Chinese noodles and topped with cashew nuts.

—Seasoning with curry powder, apples and raisins will take you to India.

—You will have a hard time convincing friends you didn't slave when you produce this Continental combination: shrimp or crab, artichoke hearts, mushrooms, sliced green stuffed olives and rice—this time with mayonnaise or equal parts mayonnaise and sour cream instead of cream sauce, and sprinklings of Parmesan cheese and paprika.

You might wonder how to collect these and other casserole recipes. You don't need recipes once you know the basic components of every casserole, which needn't follow precise proportions. In general, use approximately one part of poultry, fish or meat to one part of starch (such as rice or noodles) to slightly less than one part of thickener (such as cream sauce, cream soup, mayonnaise or sour cream or a combination).

Then your ingenuity takes command. If you add hard-cooked eggs or mushrooms, cut down the quantity of the first ingredient. Top with cheese, bread-stuffing mix, or slivered almonds. Season and garnish to suit your own taste.

Your emergency shelf, intended for unexpected guests, will serve your family beautifully those days when you can't crowd in a stop at the market.

Don't feel guilty when you dip into your reserves. They *should* be used and replaced periodically with a fresh supply because they will deteriorate if stored too long. Stack the replacements to the rear of the shelf to maintain an up-to-date rotation.

RANDOM THOUGHTS ABOUT DINNERS

1. Estimate the dinner hour from the time the first guest arrives, not the last. Sometimes guests will purposely arrive toward the end of the cocktail hour. They do not want or expect you to delay dinner, so let them take a drink to the table, if they wish.

2. If a hostess wonders how long to delay dinner for overdue guests, I would suggest phoning to see if they have forgotten. If there is no answer, wait ten or fifteen minutes, then serve dinner. Don't penalize those who came on time. When the latecomers arrive, greet them good-naturedly.

3. If a maid attends the door, she will take guests' coats or direct them to a coat room or bedroom. The hosts can stay close to the living room entrance and greet guests there; without help, hosts take care of door duty.

4. A dragged-out cocktail period kills a party. At first, guests are enthusiastic about seeing friends; later they become weary.

5. Predinner hors d'oeuvres should not be as filling as a cocktail party assortment.

6. Idea: For four or six people, place your small toaster-oven on an inconspicuous side table. Heat or toast a few appetizers at a time.

7. Give guests a little advance warning before announcing dinner.

8. Guests are sincere when they offer to help in the kitchen. If you work better alone, don't hesitate to say so.
    When clearing the table, take care of a foursome yourself. With six or more, let only one person help.

9. To watch someone attack corn on the cob is not a pretty sight, especially if it includes smeared lipstick. Save corn on the cob for family dinners or barbecues.

10. The hostess should notice if guests are eating slowly and pace her speed to theirs.

11. Hosts may encourage guests to take second servings, but not insist.

12. If there are guests of honor, the host toasts them first. Otherwise, he simply expresses his own sentiments in his own style.

13. Provide both regular and decaffeinated coffee.

14. If you like to play after-dinner games, refer to chapter 13.

   When arranging games for twelve or more guests, write on separate cards the names of foursomes or twosomes. Hand a card to one person from each group, and let him round up the rest of his table when they are ready.

15. When guests are ready to leave, go to the door with them, say good-bye, and *let them go*. Stand in the open doorway until they are out of range. Sometimes, especially in the country, the host sees guests to their cars.

   This chapter gave you samplings of different kinds of dinner entertaining. Let your dinner-party style change with your whims, moods and inspirations.

RECIPES

OLIVE-FILLED CHEESE BALLS

Cream together: 1 cup (240 ml.) grated sharp
                         Cheddar cheese
                         2 tablespoons (30 ml.) butter
Blend in: ½ cup (120 ml.) flour
                         Dash cayenne pepper

   Shape about one teaspoon dough around a drained, stuffed olive. Bake at 350° about 15 minutes. May freeze before baking. Can go directly from freezer to oven. If any are left over—which seldom happens—they reheat well.

CAVIAR MOUSSE

Elegant and *easy*, and sets in 2 or 3 hours.

½ envelope unflavored gelatin
1 tablespoon (15 ml.) cold water

¼ cup (60 ml.) boiling water
1 tablespoon (15 ml.) lemon juice
1 tablespoon (15 ml.) mayonnaise
Dash of liquid hot pepper seasoning, Tabasco or cayenne
2 ounces (¼ cup or 56 grams) caviar (I use lumpfish)
1 cup (240 ml.) sour cream
Onion juice to taste

Soften gelatin in cold water. Add boiling water and stir until dissolved. Cool slightly, then stir in everything else. Pour into bowl or stemmed 12-ounce (360 ml.) glass.

Serve with bland crackers or toast squares.

Make double the amount and use the extra for a delicious salad by itself, or combined with fruit or tomatoes.

CHICKEN CASSEROLE

4 double chicken breasts (approximately 3 pounds)
2 packages Broccolettes or short-stemmed broccoli spears (or use fresh broccoli and cut stems short)
1 cup (240 ml.) mayonnaise
2 cans Cream of Chicken soup
1½ teaspoons (8 ml.) curry powder
1½ teaspoons (8 ml.) lemon juice
¾ package seasoned bread stuffing
1 stick butter

Simmer chicken till tender. Grease a flat casserole well. Layer chicken chunks. Layer cooked broccoli. Spoon soup mixture over. Toss stuffing with melted butter. Layer on top. Bake at 350° uncovered 20 to 30 minutes. (Can be assembled the day ahead too. Add dressing before baking.) Serves 6 or 7.

"BRANDIED" FRUIT

Once you have a starter, brandied fruit lasts a lifetime and is worthy of becoming a legacy. It is decorative on your kitchen counter and ever-ready to turn a meal into a feast.

Equipment:
A glass jar, such as an apothecary jar. The lid should *not* make it airtight.

To Start:
—Drain and dice 2 cups (480 ml.) canned peaches. Place in apothecary jar.
—Stir in 2 cups (480 ml.) sugar.
—Stir every day for two weeks.
—The fruit will start to ferment, bubbles will form and create its own brandied liqueur.

Add to this mixture after two weeks, and every two to four weeks thereafter:
  —1 cup (240 ml.) drained, diced, canned fruit.
  —1 cup (240 ml.) sugar.
  —At each addition, rotate using canned peaches, apricots, mandarin oranges, pineapple, and always a few slices of maraschino cherries for color. *Never* use pears or fresh fruit.

General instructions:
  —Stir every few days and let air into the mixture.
  —Never let mixture get lower than 1½ cups (360 ml.).
  —Never refrigerate.
  —Wipe the inside of the jar neck so syrup will not make lid airtight.
  —When you have enough to spare, you can remove 1½ to 2 cups (360 to 480 ml.) to start another batch as a gift.

To serve:
  —An ever-ready sauce for ice cream, pound cake, toasted angel food cake, or over fresh fruit halves.
  —Warm the sauce, add a little more liqueur, and flame it. Delicious over crêpes, baked bananas—anything!

7. A SPECIAL MORNING COFFEE

A purely social morning coffee party is less formal than a tea, but serves the same purpose—to meet a visitor, introduce a neighbor, show off the new baby, celebrate a holiday, or for no reason except to gather friends together.

Fare can be as simple as assorted sweet rolls or as abundant as the menu I serve at my traditional, Christmas season *Shoppers' Coffee Break.*

Sixteen years ago on the second Tuesday in December, I gave my first Shoppers' Coffee Break to welcome friends to our new home. I have repeated it every year since on the same day.

Friends drop in during the morning at their convenience. If their day is crowded, they come as they are—in riding clothes, ready for golf, or on the way to the hairdresser.

I love the warmth of a family Christmastime party. Friends have learned they are welcome to bring a mother or daughter, and that I am happiest when three generations of a family come together.

A detailed description of my morning coffee party might inspire you to establish your own tradition in your own style.

1. Hours: 9:30 until 12:15. More customary hours are 10:00 to 12:00. I extended the time at both ends to give more latitude to those with morning appointments.

2. Don't count on a lunch date yourself before 1:30.

3. If you have extra help, plead, beg, get down on your knees if necessary, but ask them to arrive by 7:15. That is not too early to insure that everything will be ready for the early arrivals.

4. I used to ask for responses. Now I've reverted to the refusal formula (page 6).

5. The dining table is extended to its maximum, with tea and coffee services and pourers at each end. Close friends take pouring duties for one half to three quarters of an hour stints.

6. After the first few guests arrive, I hang my indispensable "Please Come In" sign (page 206, item 14) on the doorknob and stay near the door to greet and to say good-bye.

7. After guests hang their coats on racks in the bedrooms, they go to the living room where a fire blazes invitingly. There, a few close friends (the off-duty pourers, for example) offer them their choice of tomato juice or a bloody mary, and help with introductions.

8. This little interlude in the living room immediately sets a warm festive mood; it also helps the "circulation" of the party. Usually guests plunge into the deepest crush which in this case is the dining room. This pause by the fireplace gives time for some of those in the dining room to finish and come back to the living room.

MENU AND PLANNING

I confess that each year becomes slightly more ambitious, but not as extensive as this list might appear. I vary the menu from the following breakfast-type selections, and wouldn't consider serving them all at one party. They are merely suggestions; you may have better ideas of your own.

1. *The Mainstays:*

   —Well-seasoned tomato juice; add a little sugar too.

   —Bloody marys. Mix pitchers of them ahead of time, and add ice to each glass when serving.

   —Tiny doughnuts or doughnut holes.

—Sausages on toothpicks, kept hot in a chafing dish.

—Broiled chicken livers on toothpicks in a chafing dish or on a hot tray.

—Thin slices of ham topped with deviled egg on rye bread.

—Deviled egg mixed with crisp bacon on toast rounds.

—Pigs in a blanket (sausages rolled in croissant dough and baked).

—English muffin wedges with cheese and diced ham heated in the oven or broiler.

—Bacon sprinkled with brown sugar, baked the day before in a *very* slow oven; reheat in a low oven. As popular as this was, it is too time-consuming to prepare in large quantities; but try it for a *small* group, and also as a delicious hors d'oeuvre.

2. *For sweet-toothers:* buttered orange bread, cinnamon-toast squares made ahead and reheated, coffee cake, Christmas cookies or bite-sized fruit cake baked in tiny paper nut cups.

3. *For color and flair:* a platter or bowl of cubed fruit with toothpicks for spearing, accompanied by bowls of brown and powdered sugar for dipping. While strawberries are prettiest, if they aren't available, substitute pineapple wedges and mandarin oranges.

Additional Christmas season garnishes include spiced walnuts, stuffed dates, or candied orange or grapefruit peel.

4. *Shopping:* I always find it relatively easy to plan and shop for this sizable party. My previous records become my life line for the next party in showing me what, and how much, to buy.

By organizing the lists, as shown on page 13, I can do most of the shopping and ordering way ahead. At the very moment of reviewing my lists for this book, I was reminded that there was nothing left to buy on the preparty day except fruit and chicken livers. Even as I was finishing this book, I was able to continue my traditional party—thanks to my memory-bank lists.

5. *The Preparty Evening:* The table is completely arranged. Foil or plastic wrap covers cookies and fruit cakes, and dish towels are strategically draped over plates and coffee services. Nothing more to do but set the alarm clock!

After the pleasant morning is over, nothing is put away except the food. Cups, plates, spoons, coffee service and a new supply of napkins go right back on the table ready for the next morning's coffee party.

Although my mother always attends my coffee break and pours, I duplicate the party especially for her and her friends the following day (chapter 21).

My husband promises that one of these years he is going to invite a few gentlemen to follow my morning coffee with his own drop-in lunch. I hope he does. I'll just add a casserole.

8. BRUNCH

Think "weekend," and one automatically pictures relaxing with good friends. What better way than to give a Sunday brunch!

An informal brunch is easier on hosts than lunch or dinner—an important *plus* factor for those whose weekdays are spent at work. It is a convenient, less costly, and pleasant way to bring together friends of different groups and ages with no concern about even numbers or "pairing."

Any excuse can trigger a get-together for brunch: before or after a tennis game or to watch a special on television; an out-of-town visitor with an otherwise full calendar can probably squeeze in time for brunch.

One doesn't need an excuse to invite good friends—any number from two on. If your table will seat everyone, fine! Otherwise, guests can take their plates and sit any place, including on the floor.

HOW TO ORGANIZE A BRUNCH

I am not a morning person who wakes up singing and raring to go. Yes, I get up early, to accomplish everything I have in mind, such as finishing this book. My body moves around in the morning doing whatever I programmed it to do the night before. My mind does not catch up and begin to direct until considerably later.

That is why it is imperative that I prepare everything the day before. Try it; you will find yourself as relaxed as your guests at brunchtime.

1. Set the table as completely as if your guests were due within the hour.

2. Set up the juice and drink bar with glasses, blender, and everything else you might need.

3. Organize and refrigerate the food.

4. Spruce up the house. In the morning you have only to make beds, swish bathroom basins and put out fresh towels.

5. Get your clothes and accessories ready to jump into. Unless you are going out immediately after, here is your chance to wear your most colorful at-home outfit.

WHAT WILL YOU SERVE TO DRINK?

1. Have chilled fruit and vegetable juices ready in pitchers or individual cans.

2. Along with bloody marys, screwdrivers, and other juice combinations, you can serve mixed drinks which incorporate milk or eggs, such as silver, gold or ramos fizzes. Whatever you decide, have the necessary ingredients handy.

3. Use a strong, good blend of coffee. Plug in the pot early for the "coffee-holics." Colorful mugs are pretty and convenient to handle.

WHAT WILL YOU EAT?

A brunch menu is relatively simple but has infinite variations. Basically, it consists of juice and fruit, meat, eggs, bread and coffee.

Fruit

Chilled fruit in season can be served first, alongside, or as dessert. Scoop individual servings into small bowls or melon halves, or let guests help themselves from a bowl.

A summer selection is glorious, but don't despair when winter comes. Orange and grapefruit sections and sliced bananas are appetizing; so is hot baked curried fruit* which is delicious with ham.

Egg Dishes

1. Omelettes, waffles and pancakes require last-minute cooking and are satisfactory only when entertaining very few guests.

2. Surprisingly, eggs Benedict* can be organized the evening before for about eight guests.

3. Shirred or baked eggs* are ideal because they can be arranged in individual ramekins ready to pop into the oven for twelve minutes.

4. For a larger group, casserole egg dishes* are easiest for the hostess. They can be made ahead and need not be eaten immediately.

Meats

1. If you followed the tip on cooking bacon ahead (page 208, item 27), reheat it at a low temperature.

2. Bake or barbecue a thick center-cut slice of ham, and slice it thin. Or chop precooked ham into the baked egg ramekin.

3. Combine chicken livers with your shirred-egg dishes, or sauté them and keep hot in a chafing dish.

Breads

It is difficult to settle on one favorite bread or pastry from such a vast, available assortment: croissants, brioches, blueberry muffins, apple and cinnamon cake, sweet rolls, and names I can't pronounce or spell. Select from a bakery, frozen-food department, or make your own specialty.

To heat rolls without burning or drying out, wrap them in foil and place in a heated oven. To keep them warm, place a cover over them on a hot tray. If you don't own "keeping hot" equipment, ask Santa Claus for it.

I hope this chapter has given you a feel for a delightful way to entertain four or forty.

RECIPES

BAKED CURRIED FRUIT (Serves 4)

1 1-pound can salad fruit or fruit cocktail (or equivalent
   amount of fruits of your choice) drained
1 cup (240 ml.) light brown sugar
2 teaspoons (10 ml.) curry powder
1 tablespoon (15 ml.) flour or cornstarch

Drain fruit, reserving juice, and place in a shallow casserole.
Combine all dry ingredients and sprinkle over fruit. Dot with
bits of butter, and sprinkle with some of the reserved juice. Bake
at 350° for one hour.

BAKED EGGS

The day before, dice boiled or baked ham. Grate Gruyère or
Swiss cheese. Refrigerate in plastic bags.
In the morning, place ham in buttered ramekins, and make
two indentations. Break an egg into each. Sprinkle generously
with grated cheese, and sprinkle with paprika.
Bake at 325° for 12 minutes.

CASSEROLE EGGS

Cut hard-boiled eggs in half and remove yolks. Mix yolks
with mayonnaise or cream and season with one of the following: anchovy paste, mustard, chopped sautéed mushrooms or
shredded ham. Restuff. Put halves back together as one egg and
place in a single layer in a shallow casserole. Cover with a generous amount of cream sauce mixed with curry, cheese or sliced
mushrooms. Bake at 350° to heat through. Elegant and delicious
with barbecued or baked ham.

PREPARE-AHEAD CHEESE FONDUE

8 slices stale white bread, crusts removed
1½ to 2 pounds (680–906 gms.) sharp Cheddar cheese, grated
6 eggs
2½ cups (600 ml.) half and half
1 rounded teaspoon (9 ml.) brown sugar
1 finely minced shallot, green onion or scallion
½ teaspoon (3 ml.) paprika
½ teaspoon (3 ml.) each: dry mustard, Beau Monde seasoning, salt and Worcestershire sauce
⅛ teaspoon ground pepper
⅙ teaspoon cayenne pepper

Butter bread heavily and dice into ¼-inch squares. Butter a flat 3-quart casserole. Layer ½ bread and ½ cheese. Repeat. Beat eggs. Blend in rest of ingredients. Pour over bread and cheese *24 hours ahead*. Add more cream if necessary so it shows around edges. Lay waxed paper on casserole. Cover and refrigerate.

Remove 30 minutes before baking. Set in a cold oven in a shallow pan with ½ inch cold water. Bake one hour at 300° or until fondue is brown and bubbly.

The fondue can remain in the oven for an extra 20 minutes after it bakes, and once served, it holds well on a buffet hot tray. Delicious with pork sausages or ham.

Do ahead: The diced buttered bread and grated cheese can be stored in the refrigerator for a week, or in the freezer for many weeks.

Excellent also for lunch, supper or midnight suppers, in other words—anytime.

EGGS BENEDICT

Eggs Benedict are superb, easy and several steps can be done ahead:

—Poach eggs the day before, and float in water in a single layer. Refrigerate. In the morning, drain and cover with warm water. Let stand.
—Fry ham the day before and store in foil. Reheat in the oven.
—In the morning, toast English muffins, make blender hollandaise, and assemble.

9. LUNCH

The thought of taking time for lunch with good friends gives a sense of serenity and leisure. However, don't let tranquillity overcome you too early in the morning. Remember! Those morning hours fly by mercilessly and suddenly guests are ringing the doorbell.

Too often when one generalizes, an exception will immediately come to mind and prove the premise wrong. Nevertheless, I am daring to generalize, but taking the precaution to use the word, "usually."

Usually:

—Lunches are light, either because of a change in customs or calorie counting. Gone are heavy three-course dinner-type lunches except at formal affairs, hotel banquets, some business lunches, or for those people who want dinner at noon and a light evening supper.

—Table settings are more informal than at dinner, and lighter in feeling.

Sometimes:

—Before lunch, serve juice, thin soup or an apéritif in the living room.

Always:

—Set each place with only the necessary flatware, even if it ends up with one lonely salad fork. Dessert silver may be placed informally, as diagrammed on page 23.

—Remove candlesticks from the dining table.

—Specify at the time you invite if you wish guests to stay for games after lunch.

LUNCHEON DISHES

1. A miracle has come into my life—a cheese soufflé* to make ahead and freeze! I used to hold my breath and tiptoe around the kitchen; no longer.

2. Crab or clam bisque.* With time to shop, fresh crab makes this soup very special, but canned crab or clams are also delicious. If you enjoy it as much as I, keep the necessary canned ingredients on hand for impromptu occasions.

3. Women love salads as much for their beauty as their taste. How glamorous salads become when touched by the hostess' artistry!

   The most commonplace tuna, chicken or shrimp salad becomes a picture when served in a pineapple shell or cantaloupe cut in half with a fluting knife. When one sees an aspic ring* encircled with groupings of cherry tomatoes, avocado slices and egg halves, one realizes it is the beautiful color and arrangement that lifts it out of the ordinary.

   Even when a salad's low-calorie look is an illusion, women go along with the deception and enjoy it, conscience-free.

DROP-IN LUNCH

A delightful innovation is a luncheon served continuously over a two- or three-hour period while guests drop in and leave at will. This is a pleasant way to entertain a fairly large number of friends at one time, no matter what time of year. Besides being appropriate during the holiday season, the drop-in luncheon lends itself well to the out-of-doors in midsummer.

1. Suggested hours: 12:00 until 2:00, or 11:45 until 2:30.

2. Ladies often prefer sherry, dubonnet, or other light drinks before lunch. A deliciously refreshing and unidentifiable combination, which can be stored for days in the refrigerator, consists of 1 quart of dry sherry mixed with one 6-ounce can of frozen lemonade, thawed, and poured over ice.

3. *Menu Idea #1*

   —Choose food that will appear as attractive on the buffet table for the late-arriving guests as the early ones.

   —Suggestion: sea food or chicken dishes served from chafing dishes or casseroles.

   —An aspic salad mold, or a platter of individual groupings of salads, either vegetable or fruit. (Try canned lichee nuts filled with cream cheese and chopped crystallized ginger on fruit salad.)

   —Buttered rolls.

   —A sweet such as extra-fancy cookies, petit fours, or other pastry.

   —Tea or coffee.
   For this type of menu everything can go on one plate. Or, use mat-sized trays set with silver and napkins. Let guests sit in groups wherever they choose, but be sure to provide lots of tables for coffee and tea cups.

4. *Menu Idea #2*

   —Both the menu and arrangement are similar to a tea (page 75, item 6).

   —Set out an array of open and closed sandwiches such as crab or sliced turkey garnished with cranberry jelly cutouts. They should be larger and more satisfying than tiny tea sandwiches.

—At one end of the table, or at a separate table
nearby, place a soup tureen and mugs. Soup can
be thick or light, but for easy handling, one should
be able to drink it without having to use a spoon.*

Keep the tureen replenished for those second or
even third servings, which signify "enjoyment."

—Assortment of sweets.

WEEKEND LUNCHEONS

Some people like to entertain mixed groups at weekend
lunches instead of dinners. The noon hours are convenient
if friends have to drive some distance.

If the occasion warrants it, one can go completely formal, in which case service would follow the pattern of the
Formal Dinner, page 39. More often, lunches are informal buffets served inside, or out of doors in the summer.

The menu is similar to a Sunday supper: one hot dish,
salad, hot bread and dessert, or soup, cold poached sal-
mon and dessert.

Guests usually do not stay long afterward unless an ac-
tivity has been planned—perhaps games or even a dance.
A luncheon-dance is very festive.

Lunching on the run can never compare to even the
most unpretentious midday break with friends.

RECIPES

These delicious soups can be made a day or two ahead in the
blender and stored in the refrigerator. Most soups freeze unless
they contain cream, which should be added after thawing.

SPINACH SOUP

Blend together: 1 can vichyssoise
                  1 package *creamed* frozen spinach, cooked
                  2 tablespoons (30 ml.) Spice Islands
                     chicken stock base

Thin with milk or cream. Add *lots* of grated lemon rind, a dash
of nutmeg, and a jigger of vermouth. Serve hot or, preferably,
icy cold.

BEET SOUP (borsch without cabbage) is an excellent blender mix of 1 can of beets, including juice to 1 can undiluted consommé and 1 teaspoon (5 ml.) vinegar. Top with sour cream or whipped cream flavored with horseradish. A cateress said that using vinegar instead of lemon juice helps retain the color.

Both beet and spinach soups are equally delicious hot or chilled.

CUCUMBER SOUP should be served icy cold. Coarsely chop 1 or 1½ seedless or seeded cucumbers, sauté over very low heat with shallots (freeze-dried will do) or scallions in 2 tablespoons (30 ml.) butter about 10 minutes, but do not brown. Add all to 3 cups (720 ml.) boiling strong chicken broth and cook until softened, approximately another 10 minutes.

Then purée in a blender. Add 2 tablespoons of lemon juice and as much chopped dill as you like. (I like lots.) Whisk in about ½ cup (120 ml.) unflavored yogurt, which gives a tang. Then chill thoroughly.

As with all cold soups, taste again for seasoning *after* chilling. I suspect the reason more seasoning is often needed is that the cold dulls taste buds.

Search out and collect your own interesting soup recipes. The kind that features an exotic seasoning will defy a guest to detect that it all developed from a can of chicken broth and an apple.

CHEESE SOUFFLÉ (FREEZABLE)

3 tablespoons (45 ml.) butter or margarine
2½ tablespoons (38 ml.) flour
1 cup (240 ml.) milk
1½ cups (360 ml.) grated sharp Cheddar cheese
¾ teaspoon (3¾ ml.) dry mustard
Dash of cayenne
3 whole eggs
2 additional egg whites
½ teaspoon (2½ ml.) cream of tartar

Melt butter; blend in flour. Add milk; cook and stir until thick and bubbly. Add cheese and seasoning; stir till melted. Remove from heat. Separate eggs; beat yolks till thick and lemon colored. Stir cheese mixture into yolks; cool. Beat all egg whites with cream of tartar to stiff peaks. Fold yolk mixture into whites. Pour into four ungreased 1-cup (240 ml.) soufflé dishes. Cover airtight and freeze. To bake: Set frozen soufflés in shallow pan with ½ inch hot water. Bake at 300° approximately 1¼ hours until set.

CRAB OR CLAM BISQUE

1 can undiluted tomato soup
1 can undiluted pea soup
1 can undiluted consommé
Fresh or canned crab—a generous amount—*or*
1 can minced clams including the liquid
Sherry

Blend soups and heat. Thin with water to the consistency you like, preferably thick. Add sea food and heat thoroughly, but do not boil. Add a jigger of sherry and serve.

Accompaniment: buttered toast, sprinkled with sesame seeds. Just before serving, heat under broiler.

GRAPEFRUIT-CHUTNEY SALAD RING

2 packages lemon Jell-o
1 package lime Jell-o
4 cups (960 ml.) grapefruit juice, or blended grapefruit
    and orange juice
2 fresh grapefruit
1 cup (240 ml.) seedless grapes
2 tablespoons (30 ml.) chopped crystallized ginger
½ cup (120 ml.) chopped chutney

Cut grapefruit into sections free of membrane. Add resulting juice to canned juice.

Heat 2 cups (480 ml.) juice very hot to dissolve Jell-o; add rest of juice; stir thoroughly.

Line ring mold with grapefruit sections and pour in enough Jell-o mix to hold them in place. Add chutney, ginger and grapes to remaining Jell-o. When chilled mixture is syrupy, spoon into mold and refrigerate.

Mound the center of the ring with chicken salad. With the flavor of this aspic, I prefer the diced chicken mixed with French dressing instead of mayonnaise. I also add chopped parsley, celery, sliced water chestnuts, capers, and top with toasted slivered almonds.

10. AFTERNOONS—EVENINGS TOO—
OF BRIDGE AND OTHER GAMES

As the previous chapter on luncheons pointed out, it takes a vast amount of advance organization and fast action to be ready to greet guests by noon—and *still smile*. If you are not a morning person, it is even worse. But don't despair, settle for an afternoon party.

Besides giving more leeway, you can entertain more guests than you might conveniently handle at a lunch.

Even the bedroom makes a cozy hideaway for serious bridge or domino players, whereas that same isolated location might seem unsociable for lunch.

Although this chapter discusses a ladies' afternoon, many of the same ideas apply to one including men—in the evening or a weekend afternoon. Some thoughts specifically for men are to be found at the end of this chapter.

WHICH GAMES

The most popular games for multiples of four are bridge, dominoes and gin rummy. Mah-Jongg still rates high in some areas.

There are many two-handed games including gin rummy, dominoes, cribbage, and that fascinating speedy rage—backgammon—and competition can be fierce. Afternoon or evening sessions can be run as round-robin tournaments giving everyone a chance to play with everyone else.

If some guests will enjoy playing two-handed games, you have more latitude in the number you invite. Otherwise, invite any multiple of four. Foresighted hosts will deliberately hold themselves in reserve as alternates in case of a last-minute regret.

BRIDGE

Because bridge is the most universal game, let us detail ways to organize an afternoon of bridge. Many of the same plans will apply equally well in the evening and to other games.

Selecting Partners

If you can count on your guests being compatible, let them draw for partners and tables. Otherwise, arrange the foursomes in advance, aiming for harmonious and evenly matched groupings.

Methods of Play

1. *Rubber bridge* tends to keep together players of similar ability who like to play for the same stakes.

2. *Chicago* enables players to move and change partners after each round, which consists of four hands.

3. *Duplicate* teams play the same hands as every team. Results one could normally shrug off are recorded, compared and graded, somewhat like school exams, by giving points.

   Hesitate a long time before planning a duplicate tournament at home, unless you know for certain that players are relatively evenly matched and equally enthusiastic and competitive.

   If you decide to risk a home tournament, unless you are competent, you should hire a qualified director. Otherwise, the day could turn into a shambles.

   Team-of-Four is a comfortable variation of standard duplicate play for eight equal players. Team play does not require a director, and is fun for mixed pairs. Results can be recorded as a simple plus, minus, or tie.

   Hosts who decide on Duplicate or Team-of-Four can find booklets, charts and diagrams in book and stationery stores which explain every detail of scoring and procedure.

Progression of Players

During the course of a session, it is more sociable to progress from table to table than to play a set game with the same foursome.

However, don't expect rubber bridge players to progress to other tables, because rarely do two tables finish a rubber at the same time. Most players prefer Chicago—often called "party bridge"—to avoid interminable waiting.

Following are alternate routines and suggestions on how to progress, and many of the routines apply equally well to other four-handed games. Take your choice:

1. Place a number on each table.

2. If you want to maintain the same partnerships (more customary in competition and benefit tournaments than for home entertaining), all the players sitting in the East and West positions move to the next table regardless of winning or losing the round. Players at table #1 move to #2, #2 to #3, #3 to #4, and #4 moves to table #1.

3. Or, the partners with the high score move to the next numbered table (as explained in item 2). There they draw cards for new partners—the higher of one team to be paired with the higher of the other team.

4. Or, in order to circulate the guests even more thoroughly, one member of a team moves to the higher numbered table while the other moves to the next lower numbered table. Because they have identical scores, they can cut cards to decide in which direction to move. The explanation is simple when men and women are present, such as "High man moves up; low lady moves down." Expect to hear moans of protest from those women who resent being called "low ladies."

5. Or, buy commercial bridge tallies which contain a printed routine for individual scoring. The tally indicates each player's next position.

If you choose this system, double check the tallies before buying to be certain the routine is for the number you've invited. Tallies are available with progression for eight, twelve or sixteen players.

Scoring

To avoid confusion or dissatisfaction, specify your method of scoring. Should players record:

—Their total scores?

—Their net scores?

—If playing Chicago, will the winning score be based on total high points, or on the number of rounds a player wins?

An Odd Number

Don't panic if, in spite of your best effort, you find yourself with an incomplete number to fill out the games you planned. Last-minute emergencies often occur. So, if a guest phones to cancel, don't bristle. Some day you might have to cancel at the zero hour, so be sympathetic.

Assure her you understand and will miss her, and that you can rearrange the games.

And you can!

If you held yourself in reserve for an emergency, your problem is solved. Or try one of the good games for two or three players.

If you find yourself with five bridge players, you have these choices:

1. Rubber bridge. The player drawing the lowest card will sit out for the first rubber, which could mean hours!

2. Chicago. Players take turns sitting out the four hands that complete one round.

3. Captain and Crew. This variation of rubber bridge is an excellent solution because a player sits out for only one hand, then plays two hands.

If you are not already familiar with this routine, it is worth learning—not only for emergencies, but because it is enjoyable enough to deliberately plan a fivesome. The hostess particularly appreciates the brief snatches away from the table to attend to little tasks.

Teams: To make up the two teams, all five players draw cards. The two highest become one team called the *Captains.* The other three players form the other team called the *Crew.*

Captains remain as partners until the rubber ends; however, the other three players take turns and change at the end of each hand.

—A plays with B
—B plays with C
—C plays with A
—A plays with B again, and the rotation continues until the rubber is completed. For the next rubber, draw again for new captains and crew.

Scoring with five players: In order to balance the score, follow this procedure:

—Score each one of the three crew members first. If they win a 10 rubber, each will be plus 10.

—To figure the score of the two captains, add the three crew scores together—in this case 30. Then divide it in half. In this example, each captain would be minus 15.

—What about fractions? Yes, they sometimes occur. For example, if the three crew members are minus 7—a total of 21—each captain would score one half of 21, or plus 10½. See! No problem.

Captains either win or lose more—50 per cent more to be exact. Therefore, it is inequitable to have them in competition with tables of conventional foursomes.

Six players can divide into two teams, three to each side. Both sides follow the same rotation previously outlined for the crew. The score balances normally with three pluses and three minuses. The only catch to this musical-chairs routine is to remember which team you are on!

PRIZES

When you give a party where games are played, it is customary to provide prizes. In addition to giving prizes to the winners, some hostesses give a "consolation prize" to the lowest scorer. Appropriate prizes are:

—Cosmetic items such as elegant soap, body lotions, and bath accessories

—Every lady loves handkerchiefs

—And growing things: Plants to hang, or set on a table, terrariums, herbs or outdoor plants

—Garden accessories and tools

—Gourmet food specialties

—Purse accessories

I remember an innovative idea that added a game all its own. The ingenious hostess bought enough novel little prizes for each guest to start with one she drew from a grab bag of sorts.

Each time the players moved to a new table, the gifts changed hands by cutting cards and choosing.

Don't hesitate to dream up an original idea of your own.

STAKES

Many people like to play for stakes in addition to prizes; for others, stakes are a no-no.

It is important for the hostess to be aware of each guest's attitude toward playing for money, and to bypass a possibly awkward situation or embarrassment before it happens.

To sum up some of the hostess' choices:

1. Arrange compatible foursomes who customarily play for the same amount.

2. If she sees the need, she can avoid stakes entirely by saying, "Today we are going to play for prizes." Competition is what every game is about, and competing for a prize will satisfy guests.

3. Set uniform, moderate "house stakes" at a comfortable level for everyone.

4. Guests can put a modest amount into a kitty. Inasmuch as it is their money, let *them* decide how to divide the pot.

5. When asking a guest to substitute in a regular foursome, alert her to the normal amount of the stakes. Let her feel free to say if she would rather wait until another time when she can play for smaller stakes.

6. When players progress from table to table, they can settle up before their next move, but to save time, it is easy to post the pluses and minuses on a chart and settle at the end of the day.

WHAT SHALL I SERVE?

At an afternoon party, invite for one o'clock or one-thirty for dessert and coffee and serve soon after guests arrive. Prepare a pot of tea, too.

Some hostesses prefer serving midafternoon refreshments—sweets or small tea sandwiches, or both.

Set up a tray of ice water and perhaps plug in a coffee percolator, or offer soft drinks, iced tea or punch during the afternoon. Place a dish of candy or nuts at each table. What more could your friends want except good cards!

Some enthusiastic "bridgers," who play together regularly, emphasize the game and minimize the food.

They find it more convenient to start playing before lunch —perhaps to coincide with their children's school hours. The hostess-of-the-day serves a simple dessert and tea or coffee. Each guest brings her own "survival kit"—a sandwich or whatever her diet, taste or refrigerator suggests.

FOR MEN TOO

1. Men enjoy games of skill, chance, or amusing ones that include many players; poker is always a favorite.

2. Prizes: playing cards, games, gifts for the house or garden.

3. Food should be heartier. Add a cheese and fruit platter and serve sandwiches later in the evening.

4. Start games on a weekend afternoon at three or four o'clock. Set up a do-it-yourself bar and plates of cheese and crackers and other nibbles. After play is finished, serve a buffet supper. Because you will be busy at the game tables, prepare in advance a dish that will cook without your watchful eye. A casserole is perfect. Your guests can eat at the card tables, or in informal groups wherever they like.

11. TEAS, SHOWERS, ANNOUNCEMENTS, AT HOMES

Does an invitation to a tea sound formal? Dull? Formidable? Maybe the old-time movie version influenced you: a hostess in a flowing chiffon tea gown, dowagers in veiled hats bearing calling cards in gloved hands.

Seldom is that the true picture today. To me and an increasing number of people, teatime symbolizes a leisurely, gracious time of day. Whether in the middle or at the end of an afternoon, it signifies a time for respite with congenial, old or new friends, ending with everyone refreshed, fortified and relaxed.

No wonder teatime is experiencing a noticeable revival in popularity!

You might think tea entertaining doesn't fit your life style because you are too busy. At the same time a feeling nags at the back of your mind about a friend you've postponed seeing, always waiting for the right time, the free time. Solve the two problems together, invite your friend to tea, and at the same time rid yourself of that nagging feeling.

If you are employed, find a free moment on a weekend. If little children keep you hopping, indulge yourself while they nap. If outside activities fill your days, occasionally break them off a little earlier.

Invite a few other friends and there you are—GIVING A TEA, and enjoying it.

ASSEMBLE THESE FEW BASICS FOR A SMALL TEA PARTY

1. A tray with your best teapot, or matching tea service.

2. Sugar bowl filled with cubes or colored crystals (not granulated); sugar tongs or spoon.

3. Milk.

4. Lemon sliced thin, seeds removed, and a lemon fork.

5. Small napkins.

6. Spoons.

7. Because it is difficult to juggle a cup, saucer, and separate plate, eliminate the saucer. Use a dessert or salad-sized plate with a matching cup. Tea sets are also available with an off-center cup indentation leaving room on the plate for sandwiches and cookies.

8. Before guests arrive, pour boiling water in the tea pot and let it stand. It will take only a few moments away from your guests to steep the tea in the hot pot and bring it in. Seat yourself, pour and enjoy.

WHAT TO SERVE AT A SMALL TEA

For a simple, impromptu tea, you need serve only cookies, brownies, cinnamon toast or other hot bread, such as wedges of toasted and buttered English muffins.

Keep a mixture of sugar and cinnamon in a sugar shaker to sprinkle on heavily buttered toast. Cut the toast into strips and broil for a few seconds until it is bubbly. The mixture will come in handy other times, too—try it on applesauce and rice.

If you wish to make a few open-faced sandwiches, then add a sweet—cookies, fruit cake or candy.

As the number of guests increases so will the selection on your tea table. At the end of this chapter you will find a sample list of popular tea sandwiches.* Some keep well when made ahead.

TYPICAL OCCASIONS FOR LARGE TEAS

1. Bridal or baby showers.

2. To introduce a daughter-in-law or out-of-town friend. Guests will often reciprocate by entertaining for your honoree.

3. An engagement announcement.

4. The holiday season.

5. To honor your, or a friend's, daughter of debutante age.

6. To honor your parents on an anniversary.

 Yes, men attend teas sometimes. Merely add punch* and call it a "reception."

THE LARGE TEA

I hope you agree by now that teas are not stiff, boring affairs. Here are a few thoughts to make them even more pleasant:

1. At a small tea, one invites friends to come at a specified time. For a large tea, the invitations might state from three until five o'clock, four until six, or cover a three-hour period for a very large affair. Guests will come and go during those hours; however, count on the biggest crush about mid-time.

2. Occasionally a hostess considers staggering the hours on the invitation, inviting one group from two until three, another from three until four, and still another from four until five. Resist this temptation. Such regimentation defeats the purpose of a sociable afternoon.

3. When honoring a local friend, don't use the occasion to pay off your own obligations. Tell your honoree how many guests you can accommodate and ask for *her* guest list.

4. At large affairs, a receiving line assures that all guests will meet the guest of honor.

5. If you will be part of a receiving line and cannot stand near the door, ask a friend to assist—to greet, introduce, and direct guests toward the line.

6. When only a few people come to tea, the hostess pours, but for "A Tea," she honors several close rela-

tives and friends by inviting them to pour for half- or three-quarter-hour periods.

7. The dining table is usually used for tea. Service for pouring tea and coffee is set at one or both ends, or at a separate table if space is at a premium.

8. Candles at teatime? Old rules decree no candles before five o'clock, but if the day is gloomy and wintery, who wouldn't prefer warm candle glow to the harsh glare from incandescent bulbs.

9. Tea sandwiches, sweets, candies and nuts are arranged with artistic eye appeal.

10. Stemmed strawberries are a luxury, but so pretty. Provide small bowls of powdered and brown sugar.

11. To make lemon slices prettier, before cutting the lemon, score out lengthwise narrow wedges of skin, then slice across the lemon and remove seeds.

12. Punch* is a refreshing addition to a summer tea.

13. The tea table should be as attractive and bountiful throughout the afternoon. Assign a friend or a maid to keep it constantly replenished.

   —Add to the tea and coffee pots frequently before they become empty.

   —Take away used plates immediately.

SPECIAL-OCCASION TEAS

Announcements

An engagement can be announced in one of several ways:

   —Telling or writing close friends

   —At a family dinner

   —Through a newspaper announcement made by the parents of the bride-to-be

   —At a cocktail party or a tea

Mailed formal announcements are not looked upon with favor.

Although announcing an engagement at a tea is similar to other tea parties, decorations can be more frilly, colors softer, napkins imprinted with the names of the future bride and groom, or find other more original ways to divulge the news.

Unless distance makes it impossible for the groom's mother to attend the announcement party, she should be part of the receiving line. The bride stands between her mother and her future mother-in-law.

Showers

Bridal and baby showers are fun at any hour—lunch, afternoon or evening. They are included in this chapter because they are so frequently given in conjunction with tea.

When planning a baby shower, it is better not to surprise the mother-to-be, but to ask for her guest list of close friends.

Sometimes two or more guests will buy a needed piece of baby equipment that would be too expensive for one alone.

A bridal shower is always a happy affair and can be given by anyone except a relative of the bride-to-be. It is important to ask the bride for her guest list. In this way you can avoid asking anyone not invited to the wedding, or those already included in other showers. Also ask her color preferences so you can state them on the invitations.

Best of the following shower ideas are those which allow donors to select from a wide price range:

1. Kitchen—specify color preferences.

2. Bathroom—specify color preferences.

3. Recipes and ingredients—anything from a special herb to an appropriate mold or cooking utensil.

4. Pantry—gourmet or practical.

5. Handkerchief.

6. Paper goods.

7. Round the clock—The invitation assigns each guest an hour of the day or night. The guest selects a gift suitable for that hour. The honoree may open the gifts in order of time, perhaps starting with an alarm clock, then a bath towel or box of soap, next a coffee pot or jam jar. This is the most fun!

8. Plants and related accessories, if the couple will not have to transport them too far. Gifts can include planting supplies, pebbles, containers or macramé hangers.

9. Closet accessories. One person should co-ordinate this so everything will match.

10. Pots and pans.

11. Linen—two or more guests sometimes give jointly.

12. Lingerie—I prefer to consider this a trousseau item.

13. Crystal or china—This is too price-tagged to suit my taste and comes under the wedding-gift classification.

14. Miscellaneous.

Sometimes a groom will feel left out of prewedding festivities, but not if you plan an evening shower with gifts especially for him:

15. Gadget.

16. Household tools—screwdrivers to thumb tacks.

17. Garden tools and supplies—IF the couple will be moving into a home.

18. Bar equipment.

Debuts

Generally the young ladies opt for a boy-girl party in preference to a tea. However, mothers and grandmothers love a traditional tea party where they may see their contemporaries and meet their friends' children.

1. The invitation names the young lady, or ladies, being honored.

2. Frequently the mother and grandmother are joint hostesses and both their names appear on the invitation.

3. A receiving line is appropriate.

4. If a tea is in honor of several young ladies, each girl's mother is usually invited to stand alongside her daughter in the receiving line, if space permits.

5. In a receiving line, it is easy to blank out and forget a name—even one's best friend—so don't worry if it happens. A considerate guest will quickly give his name to jog your memory.

It is well to do some homework and review names beforehand to keep the memory lapses to a minimum.

6. As a guest are you expected to send gifts or flowers? As an honoree should you expect to receive them?

In the past, a gift of flowers—frequently orchids—was automatic. In fact, the décor, such as topiary trees or garlands of greens, was arranged ready to be interspersed with floral gifts. But customs have changed. If the invitation does not preclude gifts by stating, "No flowers or gifts," they are optional. Perhaps a quarter or a third of all guests will send gifts.

Gifts are more practical and lasting when the donor is choosing for a girl going to college or on to a career. Ideas: stationery—perfume or toiletries—picture frames or albums—scarves—decorative little boxes—novelty jewelry—purse accessories.

If you prefer sending flowers, send them the day before—there is enough excitement on the party day. Always choose an arrangement, never a box of cut flowers. Better still, select a plant which the girl can take to her new quarters.

AT HOMES

"At home from 3 until 5" is simply another way of inviting friends to tea. If the invitation states a specific date, the hostess expects a response; however, no responses are necessary if she sets regular dates—for example, every second Tuesday of the month.

My happy memories go back years to a family who served tea daily at four o'clock. The children, with a twelve-year span between eldest and youngest, brought their friends from tennis, painting or school for simple tea and buttered bread or homemade cookies.

As refreshing as the tea always was, more stimulating were the companionships and discussions of diverse interest, and appreciation for parents' all-are-welcome hospitality.

RECIPES

PUNCH   (makes 30 cups—4 ounces per cup)

Mix and store in refrigerator:
1 quart dry sherry
1 can frozen lemonade (thawed)
46-ounce can unsweetened pineapple juice

Just before serving, pour into punch bowl and add:
32-ounce bottle of ginger ale

Decorative Ice Wreath for the Punch Bowl
   Instead of a block of ice, substitute this beautiful cooler. Use a ring mold that will fit inside your punch bowl. Pour in ¼ to ½ inch of water or fruit juice and place in your freezer. Just before it solidifies, arrange a colorful layer of fruit—lime and orange slices, cherries, or whatever complements the flavors of your punch. Add more liquid and freeze again, then more fruit and continue to build up a frozen-fruit wreath.
   After it is completely frozen, unmold, wrap in plastic, and store in your freezer for weeks. The frozen wreath will chill the punch, decorate the bowl, and add to the taste.

TEA SANDWICHES

   Open-faced tea sandwiches need not be filling—only small, pretty and appealing. I have a personal aversion to unidentifiable mixtures, no matter how acceptable their ingredients. For example, I prefer slices of chicken or whole small shrimps to a ground or finely chopped version of the same ingredients.
   After sandwiches are made, they require refrigeration in single layers which often creates a serious storage-space problem. This need inspired me to devise a way to store six to eight trays in the base space of one. On pages 207–8, item 26, you will find a diagram and description of my homemade invention, which you will also find handy for storing premade hors d'oeuvres.

Tomato Aspic rounds are a colorful accent to a plate of tea sandwiches.

The day before: Make extra-firm aspic (1½ tablespoons or 23 milliliters gelatin to a pint of liquid) using highly seasoned tomato juice, blended vegetable juices or bloody mary mix as the base. Pour into a flat dish or cookie sheet to a depth of no more than ¼ inch. When set, score with the same size cookie cutter you used for the bread rounds.

Slice pimiento-stuffed green olives and store in a covered dish.

The party day: With a small spatula, place aspic rounds on bread which has a dab of mayonnaise to keep them from slipping. Decorate with an olive slice, and refrigerate.

While *Cucumber Sandwiches* cannot be made the day before, they hold up well if made early in the day. Cut cucumber slices to match the precut and buttered bread. Butter keeps these sandwiches from becoming soggy. Curry-flavored mayonnaise and a sprinkling of dill sparks their taste and looks.

Cream Cheese is the standard base for many delicious tea sandwiches. Mix cheese the day before with any of the following: chopped parsley, chutney, chopped watercress, crystallized ginger, clams or other sea food, or crumbled crisp bacon combined with chopped bell pepper—use both red and green peppers for more color or a Christmas look.

Day Before Sandwiches
Have bread cut in lengthwise thin slices at your bakery.

Pinwheels: Spread a single slice with a tasty and colorful filling such as homemade pimiento cheese or watercress butter, roll lengthwise, and wrap tightly in a towel or waxed paper, and chill. On party day, slice across in rounds.

Ribbons or Strips: Spread long bread slices, each with a different but taste-compatible filling. Stack several layers. Chill thoroughly before slicing.

Caterers count on five to six sandwiches per person, but prepare more to keep the plates filled. A representative assortment will include four to six varieties.

12.   COCKTAIL AND OPEN-HOUSE PARTIES

Cocktail parties are great fun, as we all know. Everyone has attended dozens of them, but it is amazing the questions that come to mind and the decisions that must be made when one is about to give a cocktail party of his own.

You will spend time, money, and effort—substantial amounts of each—so why waste them on a huge crush-and-din affair. If you use the occasion as a means to pay off a year's obligations, guests will not feel particularly flattered.

It is better to invest all that time, money, and effort wisely, perhaps in a series of smaller parties, where each guest is made to feel important.

Call it a cocktail party or an open house. At a cocktail party, an assortment of drinks is served. An open house can be limited to serving egg nogs, Tom and Jerrys, wine or punch. Open houses are often family affairs, and might span a longer period of time—an entire afternoon or evening if one wants.

Consider some of the options before you make your final plans.

DECIDE ON NUMBER OF GUESTS

You, alone, can decide how many guests to include at one time. In spite of previous cautioning about wall-to-wall people and intolerably high decibel levels, a party is not overlarge *provided* the home can accommodate everyone comfortably, or has a usable garden or deck to handle the overflow. A large party gives an opportunity to see friends whose paths don't often cross, and to meet new people.

—First, write down the names of those you want to invite, then decide whether or not to break the list into two or more parties. You can safely overinvite because not everyone will accept (page 6).

—If you give two or more parties, they will be more stimulating and successful if you mix groups instead of confining each party to those who see each other regularly.

THE HOURS

A two-hour period is average. Guests seldom arrive at the earliest time, unless they stop in briefly on their way to another engagement. They prefer to wait until they can visit with more friends, which means that the crunch will come in the mid-period.

You know from the pattern of your own lives which hours are best for you and your friends:

—5:00 until 7:00. A little early for business people or commuters, but satisfactory if one lives in the city and wants friends to come immediately from work.

—6:00 to 8:00. Convenient for many, even those going on to a dinner party or theater.

—6:30 to 8:30.

—7:00 to 9:00. Because of the late hour, plan to serve more substantial food, and count on people staying longer.

—5:00 to 8:00. Good hours for very large parties on weekends, or to accommodate more people in limited space.

—or best of all, 6:00 or 6:30 on, in hopes guests will stay as long as they like.

ONE MORE DECISION BEFORE YOU INVITE

Substantial food or not?

At a cocktail party or open house, hors d'oeuvres alone are sufficient, and guests expect no more. But many times at a cocktail party, hostesses bring out a buffet later in the evening for the few they have asked to stay, and others whom they invite on the spot.

This procedure is my pet peeve.

These spontaneous, well-meant invitations are sometimes misinterpreted. Guests suddenly wonder if the hosts felt obligated to invite them because they overstayed. Instead of being pleased with the invitation they become embarrassed. They either leave immediately or, if persuaded to remain, wonder if they've done the right thing.

Recommended: VIP treatment for all or none!

There are various ways to serve more than hors d'oeuvres without becoming involved in a complete buffet dinner, if you are so inclined. Only after you decide whether to serve something more are you ready to send or telephone the invitations.

INVITING

Written invitations are time-savers for large parties. Fill-in cards come in almost unlimited variety—pretty, smart, funny, simple, striking, formal, informal. Choose one that suits your own style and mood. When hosts use their first names, Susie and Bob Thompson, responses will also be informal, not in the third person.

Slightly more formal is the Mr. and Mrs. engraved card which is convenient to use, especially if it already includes the address:

Mr. and Mrs. James Perry Standish

Cocktails

Friday , June 4th

6:00 - 8:30

75 Evergreen Drive
Danville, Kansas

Rsup

Responses to this form are either notes or similar cards, but not formal, third-person answers.

Seldom does one issue formal, third-person invitations for cocktails unless it is to be a most special occasion. Even then, the party would probably be called a "Reception."

Inviting by telephone is advisable for a small party. Instant refusals will give time to substitute other names up to your desired quota.

Telephoning also gives the opportunity to explain if one wants guests (all or none) to stay on, so they won't make plans to go out to dinner.

Let us investigate some of the ways to word written invitations for that in-between fare which is not quite dinner.

What Invitations Imply

Misunderstandings occur only through words—a matter of semantics. Hosts can have in mind one meaning while guests interpret an invitation another way. For example, there is the finest line of distinction between the words,

"Cocktail-Buffet" and "Cocktails and Buffet," at least as I have seen them used.

—"Cocktail-Buffet" often refers to a continuous buffet throughout the evening. Guests go to the table as often as they like, and usually stand.

—"Cocktails and Buffet" indicates, somewhat ambiguously, that a cocktail period with hors d'oeuvres will be followed by a buffet dinner. Guests sit at tables or in groups wherever there is space.

As the recipient of an invitation with the above wordings, if you are in doubt as to their meanings, the hours will sometimes give a clue. For example, 6:00 to 8:00 or 6:00 on will signify a cocktail-type party, whereas a definite time such as 7:00 almost always means dinner.

—As hosts, try to make your plans clear. Guests appreciate knowing what to expect.

—There are many names one can call a cocktail party which provides a light buffet. Cocktails *and* hearty hors d'oeuvres; cold buffet; "small chow," a Far East expression; lap supper; finger food; et cetera; buffet supper—whatever the hosts want to call it.

"Cocktails Plus"* was a term we coined for a holiday-season party. The asterisk referred to an explanation at the bottom of the invitation which read: *"We hope you will stay for buffet if you can." We hoped our guests would infer that they were welcome for cocktails whether or not they could stay for the buffet. Evidently they were on the same wavelength and understood our message.

SERVING DRINKS

Enough preliminaries! Now, on to how best to serve drinks at a cocktail party.

One couldn't bear to hear a guest say, "How do you get a drink in this house?" Following are various ways to take care of guests' drinks.

Instructing a Bartender

Just as hosts would never say to the cook, "Cook a dinner," neither should they say to a bartender, no matter how experienced he is, "Mix the drinks." Provide him with a jigger and tell him exactly what strength drinks you wish poured. Nothing can sabotage a party faster than a bartender with too heavy a hand.

1. *Set up a serving bar* with a bartender to mix drinks. However, as the evening progresses, guests going for their drinks tend to congregate near a bar and create a bottleneck.

2. *Set up several bar stations.* This will keep people from overcrowding one area.

    In a large home, there might be as many as three bars—dining room, the entrance hall, and the living room—and a duplication of food in each room. No bottlenecks for certain!

3. *In addition to one or more bars,* waiters or assistant bartenders can circulate among the guests to take orders.

    A butler or waiter stationed near the door can immediately take orders as guests arrive. Guests should not wander too far away until the waiter returns—usually by the time a lady leaves her coat.

    Bartenders often set up a small tray with a variety of the most popular drinks to avoid that first wait. If one's preference is not on the tray, he will bring it on his next round.

4. *No set-up bar.* Drinks can be made in the kitchen or pantry *if* waiters or bartenders are available to take and fill orders.

    Bartenders must be the most observant and discerning of all men! It is remarkable how they can take a drink order and bring it to a person who has moved to the other side of the room and, also, how they can remember minute preferences from one drink to the next —just a splash—one ice cube—a twist. Don't you wonder what memory course they took?

5. *Bartender versus kitchen help.* When given a choice between the two, the consensus is for a bartender, whether a professional or moonlighter. Kitchen work can be done ahead of time, whereas tending bar could consume a host's entire evening.

6. *Pour-your-own* is an increasingly popular format. Instead of spending the evening mixing drinks for friends, a host spends it mixing *with* friends. He hospitably offers the "courtesy of the bar," but his responsibility must not end there. He needs to check the bar often to replenish ice, soda and other supplies, and encourage guests to return for refills.

Guests will fix drinks for themselves and those around them, and enter into the spirit of a do-it-yourself party.

STOCKING THE BAR

We have such a phobia about running short that we always oversupply, but nothing is lost or wasted. If one wants to decrease his inventory after a party, most bottle shops will take back the surplus for credit or exchange.

Discuss returns with the store manager in advance. If you bought at a discount price, you might decide to store the extra for future use.

1. Remember to provide all the soft drinks and mixes. Ginger ale is a favorite alternate for those who prefer non-alcoholic beverages. It is a good idea to have assorted single-serving juices on hand. If even one person should ask for grapefruit juice, how satisfying to be able to fill his order! The leftover juices will be fine for breakfast, or as a base for gelatin salads.

2. Wine is increasingly popular, often served over an ice cube or two. After a recent party, a hostess told me that requests for wine outnumbered orders for hard liquor two to one! Provide both white and red wine—much more white—in half or full gallons, and transfer to decanters if you wish. Add sherry, dubonnet, and vermouth to your list of provisions. Remember, wine glasses should be only partially filled.

3. Don't forget beer.

4. Scotch, bourbon, vodka and gin are standard in most parts of the country, rum in some areas. As to amounts, count on a fifth to serve about six persons, a quart to serve seven. However, because it is difficult to know which variety will have a run on a particular evening, it is necessary to have plenty of each kind to spare. A bottle of wine should serve five drinks.

5. Lemons, limes, stuffed green olives, cocktail onions, toothpicks, a knife and a jigger.

6. Coasters and ash trays everywhere—even in unlikely places.

7. Cocktail napkins.

8. Wine glasses, bar glasses. Figure on many more than one glass per person. Guests often place their glasses down, forget where, then order a fresh drink.

To Buy or Rent Glasses?

Most people rent bar glasses for a large party. It is only after renting several times that the light dawns, "If I had bought them in the first place, I would have owned them by now."

So it is with all rentals. I rented coat racks four different times before I realized I could have bought two racks for the amount I had already spent. Now, belatedly, we've bought our own.

If you have enough storage space, you might look for glasses on sale, and invest in a large supply. It is convenient to have an ever-available supply without the bother of arranging delivery and pickup, and, in time, one is money ahead.

It is impossible to stock a quantity of every size glass for home use. Low, wide bar glasses and all-purpose eight- or ten-ounce wine glasses can take care of most types of drinks. For after dinner one can add brandy and liqueur glasses and, in time, other stemmed ware if one's life style calls for them.

WHAT TO SERVE

Hors d'oeuvres

If you like appetizers as much as I, you will start collecting recipes. Entire books are devoted to every conceivable kind of delicious tidbit. Depending on your plans —whether doing a party by yourself, with help, or turning the entire job over to a cateress—you will find many varieties to suit your taste.

If doing the party by yourself, look for appetizers that can be made ahead* and refrigerated on stackable trays (pages 207–8, item 26). Avoid the "pop under the broiler" variety, unless you actually like spending your time in the kitchen while everyone else is being sociable.

Caterers estimate approximately four hors d'oeuvres per person during a one-hour, predinner cocktail period, and ten to twelve per person at a cocktail party. I don't know if those estimates are trustworthy when I am present.

A Few Supper Suggestions

1. A cocktail buffet for twenty-four—without help. I fell into this party by accident the first time. It turned out to be so successful that I have repeated it several times. My "memory bank" records of the menu, amounts used, and even a diagram of the buffet and bar table settings have further simplified preparations.

The first occasion stemmed from an impulsive suggestion to come for drinks following a mixed golf tournament and then go out to a no-host dinner. The day before, I realized no one would be in the mood to go out to dinner after our athletic day. The problem narrowed down to this: How could I cope with substantial food for twenty-four without giving up my own golf game?—an alternative I didn't seriously consider.

Instead of undertaking an overwhelming amount of cooking, or wasting time trying to locate non-available help, I ordered meats roasted-to-order from a fine delicatessen. The same establishment also prepared cheese balls and beautifully decorated fresh pâté.

My only efforts were to butter assorted breads, make a caviar mousse, a roquefort quiche which is almost as good cold as hot, place little sausages in a chafing dish with a spicy chili sauce and prepare raw vegetables and a curry dip. Total time: less than an hour.

This was not a "Budget Special," nor was it intended to be. It was my solution to pulling a party together in less than a day, play golf, and be as relaxed as our guests.

However, this pattern of hunger-satisfying food need not be extravagant if one has time to co-ordinate it over a period of time. Business men and women, who have little time to make dozens of individual appetizers, find a menu of heartier food easier to prepare and serve.

Delicious sherried or brandied cheese* improves if made days ahead.

If one doesn't want to roast meat, then serve steak tartare. It *must* be fresh, and is special, hearty, quick, and stretches far.

2. "Cocktails, Quiches and Crêpes" one invitation stated. After other hot and cold canapés, the quiches and crêpes were delicious and filling. Confirmed meat-and-potato addicts planned to go out afterward, but most guests were more than satisfied.

3. Cocktails and Middle East Buffet. The hostess, who said she was weary of the "turkey-ham route," created this unusual and splendid menu based on warmed Arabian pocket bread to fill at will. When Arabian pocket bread comes from its one-minute trip on a belt through a 750° oven, it is puffy, but as it cools it flattens and resembles a thick six-inch pancake. When cut across, the thin crusts separate to form a pocket.

An interesting and delicious assortment of fillings included shrimps, chopped lamb, chicken, mashed avocado and egg salad to combine or take singly. An enormous sectioned condiment dish provided chopped tomatoes, shredded lettuce, chopped green onions, chutney and other delicacies.

Assorted fruit kabobs topped with enormous strawberries radiated from a ball of styrofoam placed in a deep silver punch bowl. Coffee and baklava completed the delicious, exotic supper.

4. Individual plates instead of a buffet. As the evening progresses, waiters or waitresses offer individual plates served from the kitchen. A creamed dish is best; for example, turkey Tetrazzini, crêpes, filled patty shells or individual shells of baked sea food.

COCKTAIL DANCE

This affair will probably take in a span of three to four hours.

Engage a band that plays "your kind of music," or if the party includes several age groups, ask the bandleader to vary the music enough to please everyone. If you also ask him to keep the dances short, people will mix better.

As soon as one or two couples start to dance, others will follow. You might have to conspire with a few close friends to set the example.

People are accustomed to standing at a cocktail party, but at a cocktail dance, they appreciate as many tables and groupings of chairs as space permits. Tables call for cloths and flowers.

In addition to hors d'oeuvres, a small buffet will be expected.

AN ATTITUDE, A POINT OF VIEW, NOT AN EDICT

Some advisers stress the various tricks, excuses, and deceptions hosts can use to get rid of guests who stay more than briefly beyond the stated hours.

My husband and I take exactly the opposite viewpoint. We consider some of those after-party, shoes-off visits the warmest, most cherished part of an evening. For us it is a time to *wind down slowly,* instead of *being let down quickly* after a mass exodus.

A very successful hostess, judging by the pleasure she gives, says, "I set a time when people can arrive, but never indicate in any way when they should leave." No wonder she is considered a glorious hostess!

An exception: If entertaining before another affair in which all guests are included, you might have to warn about an approaching deadline.

RANDOM THOUGHTS

1. Apartment dwellers do not always have space to store an extra folding table. Improvise a bar table by using a folding ironing board. Protect the pad with a piece of plastic. Then cover it to the floor with a cloth. If you expect to use this arrangement again and again, it might be worth making a permanent cover. Home-decorating books diagram how to make a fitted cover with a pleated or tailored floor-length flounce.

2. In the mistaken name of "generosity," never make superstrong drinks. It is unkind to unsuspecting guests —even dangerous.

3. Never question or notice a guest's choice of drinks.

4. If a guest is not well—no matter what the cause—it is up to the host to arrange his safe transportation home.

And finally, foresighted hosts learn they must eat something substantial *before* their open houses. A little nibbling during the party won't sustain them.

RECIPES

Our freezer always holds three kinds of hors d'oeuvres ready to go directly from freezer to oven. They are a boon for spur-of-the-moment guests, or as a head start toward a party:

OLIVE-FILLED CHEESE BALLS (See page 47.)

MUSHROOM ROLLS:

Sauté chopped mushrooms, roll jelly-roll fashion in thin bread and freeze. To serve: Cut rolls into 1-inch pieces and bake until bread browns.

ARTICHOKE CANAPÉS

2 jars marinated artichokes, 6 ounces (180 ml.) each
1 bunch green onions, chopped
Sprig of parsley
4 eggs
12 soda crackers crumbled
8 ounces (240 ml.) sharp cheese grated
Salt   Pepper   Dash of Tabasco

Fry onions in a little oil from artichoke jar. Beat eggs and add other ingredients. Chop artichokes and add to mixture.

Pack into 8-by-8-inch well-oiled pan and bake at 325° for 35–40 minutes. Cool and freeze if you wish. Cut in 1-inch squares and reheat to serve.

Other appetizers, some to make two weeks ahead, others the day before the party:

CHICKEN LIVER PÂTÉ—made prettier and tastier by molding in a thin layer of aspic made from consommé, seasoned with sherry. Unmold when firm and keep refrigerated until time to transfer to a plate with melba toast or bland crackers.

CHEESE LACE WAFERS can be stored for two weeks or more in a tightly covered can and are unbelievably easy to make.

Cut bars of Monterey Jack cheese the size of a stick of butter. Slice *very* thin—the thinner you slice it the smaller the wafer will be.

Place the squares on an *ungreased*, non-stick cookie sheet. Bake at 375° until golden and hole-y. That is all there is to it. No flour, no mixing. Watch them bubble as the moisture cooks away and leaves them lacy-looking—and *round!*

CREAM CHEESE-CHUTNEY BALLS—just mix and refrigerate. When firm, shape and roll the balls in chopped walnuts, toasted almonds or pine nuts. Refrigerate again. Serve on toothpicks or pretzel sticks.

CHAFING-DISH COMBINATIONS

Check your cookbook for a recipe to assemble ahead and serve in a chafing dish with assorted chips.

APPETIZER CASES to make a week or two ahead and fill the day of the party:

With a fork, mix room-temperature cream cheese, the barest amount of cream, a dab of mayonnaise and seasoning. The mixture should be soft enough to force through a pastry tube but still retain its shape.

Cut thin bread into small rounds or rectangles approximately 1½ by ¾ of an inch.

Spread the cream cheese mix lightly over the bread. Then carefully edge each one with a fine-tipped pastry tube—as though decorating a cake.

Freeze on cookie sheets. When hard, store in airtight bags.

Several hours before the party, remove from freezer and immediately fill the centers. Filling suggestions: red or black caviar, small shrimps, anchovies.

Place immediately on a tray, cover with plastic wrap and refrigerate. They will thaw by serving time and still be appetizingly cold.

CREAM CHEESE mixtures and suggestions are on page 82. Use the same combinations for appetizers, or thin with cream and mayonnaise for dips. Thin with lemon juice and season with onion juice to serve with caviar.

The two following cheese recipes require at least two days in the refrigerator to blend the flavors. Ten days to two weeks is not too much. Bring to room temperature to serve.

BRANDIED CHEESE

1 pound (448 gr.) grated sharp Cheddar cheese
1 8-ounce (224 gr.) package cream cheese
1 4-ounce (112 gr.) package bleu cheese
1 cup (240 ml.) brandy
1 teaspoon (5 ml.) each: dry mustard, hot pepper sauce,
    and Worcestershire sauce

Beat all ingredients for 1 minute at slow speed. Then beat at high speed for 5 minutes.

CAVIAR MOUSSE (See page 47.)

SHERRIED CHEESE

1 pound (448 gr.) grated sharp Cheddar cheese
3 tablespoons (45 ml.) each: parsley, chives and sherry
2 tablespoons (30 ml.) each: butter and Worcestershire
    sauce
Salt to taste

Mix all ingredients with electric beater until smooth. Put in crock or glass container in refrigerator.

BACON AND YOU-NAME-IT

The day before, wrap wafer-thin bacon around pitted olives, water chestnuts, dates or you-name-it. Bake in a slow oven until the grease is drained, then refrigerate on your stackable cookie sheet (page 207). To serve: Bake to heat through.

13. DESSERT

This is a simple but cordial way to entertain either a large or small group of friends, or even another couple, without undertaking an entire dinner.

TYPICAL DESSERT OCCASIONS:

1. To show pictures.

2. An evening shower for a couple, or for a bride-to-be who works.

3. Charades or other so-called parlor games.*

4. Bridge or other games.

5. Conversation with a congenial group.

Maybe you would be reluctant to invite some guests to dinner and others to dessert only. A ticklish situation? Perhaps. However, one can conceive of times when an invitation to dessert only, would be understandable. For example, a dinner for visiting relatives or close friends, with other friends to join you later. An explanation such as ". . . We're sorry we can't ask everyone to dinner, but we'd love you to join us for dessert . . ." should leave no hurt feelings in its wake. One warning: Be sure to time your dining so you will be finished and ready for the dessert contingent.

For an evening of games or pictures, make your plans clear when you invite, or guests might straggle in late. Set a realistic time—possibly 8:30, depending on distance or commuting schedules.

A COUPLE OR TWO

Set the dining table or a card table if you wish, or sit comfortably in the living room.

Serve regular or decaffeinated coffee and your favorite dessert. If you want to be particularly festive, serve a flambé dessert: crêpes suzettes, cherries, bananas or mixed fruit over ice cream, or broken macaroons soaked in wine.

The secret of successful flaming is to have everything *well-heated*—sauce, spoon and brandy or other liqueur.

Crêpes are always impressive, but so is the most ordinary canned or fresh fruit when flamed.

Suzettes pans and chafing dishes are beautiful in themselves, but not essential. Fruit may be heated in an ovenproof dish and brought to the table to flame.

PERHAPS A DOZEN

Serve whatever you make best. Some hosts like to sit at the dining room table; however, unless everyone arrives at the same time, this plan can become unwieldy. Not that people are impatient for dessert, but they may yearn for a cup of coffee.

An offer of after-dinner drinks might be welcomed after dessert.

A LARGE GROUP

A dessert buffet can be colorful and varied. Let guests select whatever, and as much as, they like. They will stand or sit in groups, and should be encouraged to return to the table often.

On several occasions I have served the following assortment, and found it was varied enough to suit all tastes:

—One sinfully rich dessert

—Assorted colors and flavors of ice cream scoops, with

nearby bowls of sauces, nuts, whipped cream and
cherries

—Lady fingers, split and filled with chocolate-flavored
whipped cream

All the above were for the sweet-toothers, but for my
taste:

—Colorful fresh fruit—figs, strawberries, pineapple
cubes, papayas.
  Suggestions for serving fruit: presented pinwheel
style or in pie-shaped sections on a flat platter; melon
balls in scooped-out, fluted watermelon half; kabobs
made by impaling an assortment of four or five bite-
sized pieces on bamboo skewers.
  Some guests combine fruit with ice cream into
magnificent jeweled towers of goodies.

—Five varieties of cheese (be sure to include some mild
ones), assorted crackers and sliced apples.

—Irish coffee.* Never underestimate its attraction.

"PARLOR GAMES"

Every now and then, parlor games are worth rein-
troducing for a change of pace, if you think your guests
will enter into the spirit.

Books of adult games can be found in bookstores, toy
departments and libraries. Some of the games and trick
questions* are hilarious. Have a supply of sharpened pen-
cils and reams of paper handy. Select games that are fun—
not I.Q. tests, nor those that call for a shy person to per-
form in the limelight.

Charades, or "The Game," is marvelous fun for competitive and imaginative people. Between sessions they can
search out stumpers for their rivals.

Rules and procedures are available for many other television games.

DROP-IN DESSERTS

There are times when you might like friends to drop in for dessert, but not necessarily spend the entire evening. For example:

1. To meet or have a reunion with a friend from out of town.

2. Welcome a newcomer to your neighborhood.

3. Introduce the new clergyman.

4. Meet a political candidate.

5. Discuss a civic problem.

6. If everyone rushed through dinner to be on time for a school "Open House," they might enjoy dropping in for dessert on their way home.

Instead of inviting for a set time, the hours could be for any time *after* 8:00, 8:30, or 9:00. A dessert buffet is ideal for a drop-in evening, but can be simplified to any degree you wish.

RECIPE

IRISH COFFEE

My recipe is a variation of the usual one. I use brownulated sugar. Purists, suit yourselves. Near the piping hot, strong coffee, set up Irish coffee cups or glasses with 1 teaspoon brownulated sugar and 1 jigger of good Irish whiskey. Add coffee and top with lightly whipped cream. Test it before you take my word; you may prefer the conventional recipe.

Have empty cups for those who prefer plain coffee without the Irish influence.

PENCIL AND PAPER GAMES

Memory Game

How many of the twenty-one states that end in "a" can you name in five minutes?

Arizona	South Dakota	Montana
Alabama	Florida	Nebraska
Alaska	Georgia	Nevada
California	Iowa	Oklahoma
North Carolina	Indiana	Pennsylvania
South Carolina	Louisiana	Virginia
North Dakota	Minnesota	West Virginia

Trick Questions

1. How many four-cent stamps in a dozen?

2. How many birthdays does the average man have?

3. Some months have thirty days, some have thirty-one, how many months have twenty-eight?

4. If you went to bed at eight o'clock at night and set the alarm to get up at nine o'clock in the morning, how many hours' sleep would that permit you to have?

5. Is it legal in the United States for a man to marry his widow's sister?

6. Do they have a fourth of July in England?

7. How many animals of each species did Moses take on the Ark with him?

8. If you had only one match and entered a room in which there was a kerosene lamp, an oil heater, and a candle, which would you light first?

9. A woman gave a beggar fifty cents. The woman is the beggar's sister, but the beggar is not the woman's brother. How can this be?

10. Why can't a man living in Winston-Salem, North Carolina, be buried west of the Mississippi?

11. You take two apples from three apples and what would you have?

12. How far can a dog run into the woods?

13. A rooster, facing north, lays an egg on a pointed roof. Which side would it roll down?

14. A man builds a house with four sides to it. It is rectangular in shape. Each side has a southern exposure. A large bear comes wandering by. What color is the bear?

15. A farmer had seventeen sheep. All but nine die. How many are left?

16. If a doctor gave you three pills and told you to take one every half hour, how long would they last?

17. In baseball or softball, how many outs in each inning?

18. An archeologist claimed he found some Roman gold coins dated 46 B.C. Is this possible?

Answers to Trick Questions

1. Twelve.

2. One.

3. They all have twenty-eight.

4. One.

5. No, a dead man can't marry.

6. Yes. They don't celebrate it.

7. None.

8. The match.

9. Beggar is the sister.

10. Because he isn't dead.

11. Two.

12. Halfway. After that he runs out of the woods.

13. A rooster doesn't lay an egg.

14. A white Polar bear.

15. Nine.

16. One hour. (Take one immediately.)

17. Six.

18. No. They couldn't know the date of Christ's birth.

14. MIDNIGHT SUPPERS

Midnight suppers are especially festive because they are something *extra*—unlike our routine, three meals a day.

If you've had a wonderful time at a dance and wish the evening wouldn't end, bring home a few friends for a late-supper snack. Or call it an early breakfast. It is also fun to plan a late supper after a concert, theater, sports event, dance, or for committee members you worked with on a club party.

IMPROMPTU

If this is a completely spontaneous invitation, you will have more kitchen volunteers than you need. Working together, it will take only moments to whip up your impromptu fare.

1. Scrambled eggs or omelettes are the standbys and, for some unaccountable reason, are always more delicious at midnight than early in the morning. Toss in grated cheese or herbs, if you wish. Along with toast and something to drink, there you are.

2. Another satisfying quickie meal is canned onion soup, made richer with extra powdered-beef-stock base, topped with toast and sprinkled with Parmesan cheese —a late evening tradition in France.

3. Cheese fondue and rarebit are both easy to make, but not as easy as taking them out of the freezer.

PLANNED AHEAD

This is one time you will literally "re-enter the scene as a guest," at the same time as your invited guests, so have everything ready to go. Make your buffet table festive by following the theme of the event you've attended, or carry out your own inspiration. There are no rules to limit you.

Menu Suggestions:

1. There is no more delicious casserole for a late supper than the cheese fondue recipe on page 57. You need look no further if your oven has an automatic timer. If not, remember it takes an hour to bake.

2. If timing is a problem, look up recipes for other casseroles that require less cooking time, or that can be cooked in advance and reheated.

3. Crêpes may be made weeks ahead and frozen. Fill them the day of the party and top with sauce. They will heat in fifteen or twenty minutes. Crêpes can be filled with sea food, chicken, ham, tuna or mushrooms, and can be bland or spicy depending upon the sauce.

4. Cream sauce dishes heat quickly in the top of a double boiler.

5. Fondue pots with their blazing burners are a decorative touch to any party. Fill the pots with traditional Swiss fondue or any of its variations, bring out a bowl of crusty French bread cubes, and the midnight supper becomes an eye-catching treat.

    Count on no more than six people for each fondue pot.

6. Serve tureens of thick soup accompanied by paper-thin sandwiches made ahead and kept fresh in foil.

7. Traditional French quiche or any of its many variations is always delicious with salad.

The late party is an extra dividend—more time to enjoy good friends and good food. When you go to bed, forget to set the alarm clock.

15. BARBECUES AND PATIO PARTIES

When guests arrive and whiff the tantalizing aroma of meat cooking over charcoal, the party is off to a good start. It feels like a "party," even for four. A lovely, informal party!

People are immediately drawn toward the barbecue. Whatever it is that entices them—the aroma, the fire's warmth, the hypnotic revolving rotisserie, or the sounds of fat popping against hot coals—guests become absorbed.

Then a strange phenomenon occurs. Friends, who wouldn't think of directing your cooking in the kitchen, suddenly become advisers and experts. The fire has too much or too little charcoal . . . the meat should be turned or shouldn't. But then, involvement is half the fun!

To keep the "experts" occupied, supply skewered tidbits for them to grill as appetizers: marinated prawns and pineapple cubes, chicken teriyaki, mushrooms and cherry tomatoes, separated by pieces of bell pepper or onion.

LOCATION ISN'T EVERYTHING

Anyone can become a barbecue addict without a steersized pit, or even a patio.

Sophisticated new barbecue equipment does everything but carve. However, meat cooked on that glorious metal monster could taste no better than when broiled on an hibachi or portable grill. Besides, where could one store or use the monster in a city apartment?

City dwellers, look to the little grill. Place it inside the fireplace or on the balcony. Use colorful everyday dishes, paper napkins; sit on the floor or at a table, and there you are, creating a new trend toward the "indoor" patio.

TIME OF DAY

This book is for everyone—everywhere—therefore, no single statement can apply to everyone's climate. You know your own locality and its weather caprices, and can schedule your patio party for the comfortable time of the day. Guests should not have to sit huddled in coats if the evening suddenly turns cold or windy.

Portable outdoor heaters (portable by two strong men) are a comfort. Each heater consists of a stand, a stem which contains its own butane, and a shield to direct the heat down. These heaters can turn improvised rooms, such as a garage, tent or canopied area, into pleasant places. One can rent heaters from party equipment and electrical suppliers, and from some florists.

If you cannot depend upon eating out of doors in the evening, plan from the start on a midday meal, or cooking outside and eating inside. If you select midday, set tables in the shade or provide umbrellas.

MENU IDEAS

1. Charcoal-broiled steaks are delicious but we prefer something that cooks longer and has time to absorb the wonderful smoky flavor.

2. Leg of lamb in any form is our favorite—boned, rolled and cooked on the rotisserie, "butterflied" and broiled, bite-size pieces on skewers, or thick lamb steaks.

3. Poultry, spareribs, fish, hot dogs and ham cook slowly; all are delicious.

4. Spareribs can be partially cooked in the oven a day or two ahead, then finished with a flourish on the barbecue.

5. A patio party is not necessarily a barbecue. Make it as simple as you want, from the proverbial cold meat or

sandwich platter with potato salad, to the most elegant glazed chicken breasts (Try them!) or lobster salad.

6. Sangria is a delicious, light fresh-fruit-and-wine punch which complements summer al fresco lunching.

Search out some of the excellent barbecue books, especially those written by Californians, to whom cooking out of doors is a way of life. The books include marvelous and unusual accompaniments to heat in the oven until the meat is ready.

ADDED SUGGESTIONS

1. Plunge bottles of drinks into a wheelbarrow or tub filled with ice.

2. To save unnecessary steps, use baskets or trays to carry everything from kitchen to patio. Remember the little things, such as bottle openers, servers, and asbestos gloves.

3. Set up an outdoor buffet table. Cover food with nylon net, or use individual mesh covers. Some covers fold like an umbrella for easy storage.

4. For picnic informality, use pottery dishes, or throw-aways—the won't-collapse kind.

5. For a change, consider individual casseroles instead of one large one.

6. Don't serve gelatin salads or desserts at midday. They melt!

7. When your chef says, "It's ready," he means NOW. Ask him to give you at least a five-minute warning.

8. For an informal eat-when-you-want patio lunch, we set out the lacquer lunch boxes we brought from Japan. The lacquer resembles tortoise shell. One sees them in Japan on trains, at shrines, or the theater, filled with

little rice cakes encased in seaweed, fish or other beautifully arranged native foods.

We pack ours with Americanized individual lunches: a chicken breast in one section, salad in another, a roll and relishes in the third. Or more simply: sandwiches, salad and cookies.

Any attractive boxes will do for guests to take to an inviting spot when hunger or the spirit moves them.

Barbecues mean comfortable, gracious, outdoor entertaining—hurray for summer!

16. PICNICS AND TAILGATING

A picnic depends upon an *attitude* rather than a *location*. It represents a change of pace, freedom and relaxation from conventional ways.

There are many ideal picnic locations to entice you—alongside a running stream, in the shade of an age-old tree, on a lake or sea shore, and at the tailgate of your station wagon in the countryside.

But, if the day is rainy, you can produce a picnic on your living room floor—as long as you maintain your same picnic attitude. Toast marshmallows and popcorn in your fireplace, and let the ants forage for themselves in the country.

The most avid picnicker I know is a charming young city dweller who expects her companions to share her enthusiasm. It's a demerit for one who doesn't.

My same adviser relishes a bit of elegance with her picnics. She says:

—"It's just as easy to pack inexpensive real wine glasses, or plastic if you must. Drinks taste better."

—"I use my colored-handled kitchen flatware."

—"Colorful permanent-press napkins—even a tablecloth—make a picnic special."

Whether you follow her advice or stay with paper napkins and plastic forks, anticipate a happy day and it will be.

Spoilage is a vital concern, so plan your food carefully. If food must go unrefrigerated for any length of time, avoid mayonnaise, cream sauces or custard fillings. However, cold chests and inexpensive styrofoam containers are readily available or can be improvised by using a plastic wastebasket or a carton. Chill with ice or a camper's reusable coldpack.

Other Tips and Suggestions:

1. Remember thirst-quenching soft drinks. Select them in bottles with screw tops or in cans with pull tabs.

2. Prefer red wine to white. It needs no chilling.

3. French or Italian bread broken off the loaf is delicious with cheese. So are rolls. Both are preferable to sliced bread which dries out quickly. However, if young children prefer conventional sandwiches, butter the bread and wrap it in foil.

4. Roasted lamb and beef keep better in warm weather than processed meats.

5. Try fried chicken, home cooked, grilled at the picnic site, or bought by the basket en route.

6. Lettuce wilts quickly. Unless you have a cooler, do without it.

7. Take your kitchen cutting board for double duty: cutting, and a sturdy surface on which to arrange and serve food.

   Any of the following can be prepared the night before:

8. Wash and cut raw vegetables. Wrap in foil which, at picnic time, becomes a "silver" serving dish.

9. Pack cut fruit in a wide-mouth thermos jug or Mason jar. Serve in plastic cups.

10. Wedges of melon are delicious if cold.

11. Neither German nor French potato salads* incorporate mayonnaise, and both are delicious.

12. Stuff hard-boiled eggs by mixing the yolks with mustard and herbs instead of mayonnaise. Put the halves back together again and pack them in an egg carton for transporting and serving.

13. Cooked artichokes can be packed in individual berry baskets which are handy to eat from.

Additional Take-alongs:

—Jug of water

—Blanket or plastic ground covering

—Packaged throw-away washcloths

—Insect repellent

—Cushions

—Eating utensils if needed

—Knife

—Sun hats or beach umbrella

—Corkscrew. Should you forget one, here's how to improvise: To remove a cork, wrap the lower part of the bottle heavily with whatever cloth is handy—a beach towel or sweater. Hold the bottle at right angles and tap the base gently against the tree. With patient tapping, in time the cork will work itself out without breaking the bottle.

If you expect to do on-the-spot cooking, look for one of the handy throw-away barbecues. It is complete with grill, frame, and briquets treated for instant starting.

TAILGATING

A crisp fall day and football calls. What better time for a tailgate feast, the ultimate in adult picnics. Leave home early to find a good parking place, then dawdle over lunch.

Tailgating can be dressed up or down. We were feeling quite dressed up and pampered at such a picnic when our hostess spread a linen cloth across the tailgate before setting out a splendid array. Then we looked around; compared to some tailgaters we suddenly felt underprivileged.

Dotting the parking lot, colorful tables were set with flowers to match the teams' colors, and even candelabra.

One-upmanship is the name of the game, and competition is fierce.

Temper your imagination only by the need to provide substantial food since the outdoors tends to whet appetites. Suggestions:

1. In addition to the picnic equipment already mentioned in this chapter, a sturdy, compact hibachi or safari grill is ideal for grilling skewered meats. How good they taste out in the open!

2. A sandwich menu can be sophisticated. Cookbooks provide all sorts of different ideas, such as rolls of marinated roast beef on French bread, open-faced sea food with Scandinavian overtones, or spicy ground meat with assorted garnishes.

3. Try a tray of assorted meat, cheeses, sea food and vegetables (covered securely so it reaches its destination intact), giving guests a chance to use *their* imagination.

4. Cast-iron casseroles, brought hot from home, will stay that way for several hours if wrapped in layers and layers of newspaper—the more the better—then in a heavy beach towel.

5. Meat pies can suggest a theme for your outing. Make them Spanish, Russian, or stay American. The secret of their diverse origins is in their seasoning and spices.
   Then serve Spanish gazpacho, Russian borsch or American cucumber soup kept icy in a thermos jug.

6. Another foreign dish worth adopting is Arabian pocket bread to fill at will (page 93). Keep the bread in the shade in plastic or foil; if it dries out it becomes too crisp to fill, although it is still good to eat alone.

7. For dessert serve fruits and a sweet that guests can pick up with their fingers.

8. Now it's your turn at one-upmanship: Irish coffee—the perfect prelude for that cool afternoon in the stadium. You already have the coffee. Just include granulated sugar and Irish whiskey, and pack a container of whipped cream in the ice chest.

Just as a picnic depends upon an attitude, so does tailgating. If you haven't a station wagon, use the hood of the car, the trunk, bring tables or spread a blanket on the ground. No matter; it's still tailgating.

RECIPES

FRENCH POTATO SALAD

Peel, slice and boil new potatoes. Drain. While warm, add a little undiluted canned consommé and white wine. Let absorb. Add a dressing of equal parts wine vinegar and olive oil, a dab of Dijon-type mustard, tarragon, salt and fresh ground pepper. Pour over potatoes and mix gently. Garnish with minced parsley.

Refrigerate only if keeping overnight. The salad tastes better at room temperature, which makes it perfect to take on a picnic.

Create other versions of non-mayonnaise salads by omitting consommé and wine, and varying the seasoning in the dressing. Try substituting lemon juice for vinegar and adding lots of dill. It's delicious.

Another version: To boiled potatoes, gently mix in cubed cucumber, thinly sliced green onion, and ripe olives.

Kitchen Tip: After boiling potatoes in their skins, submerge them immediately in cold water to arrest further cooking.

17. CHILDREN'S PARTIES

Here in mid-book, let us depart from adult entertaining to take up this very happy subject—parties for our children.

Each year is a gala occasion and each is different. As the years unfold, this difference is what makes children's parties a never-ending source of fascination to both children and parents. Let us hit the high spots of a child's progression through the years.

FIRST BIRTHDAY

How memorable that first birthday is to the parents! True, all the loving preparations are for the baby, but mothers read the pastel Happy Birthday wishes on the decorated cake; mothers blow out the solitary candle while making a wish for baby; mothers admire gifts while chubby little hands blissfully crinkle the wrappings.

Use your flash camera to record this special moment and before long even a little tot can point to himself in the photos taken when he was a baby. After seeing the pictures again and again, he almost believes he can remember his own first party.

TWO TO FOUR YEARS

Ages are approximate. Throughout his life, each child is an individual, not a digit in a bracket.

During these years, children become aware that the festivities are for His Day—the candles are his to blow, the presents his to open.

A Party

1. Arrange the party around naps and keep it brief—one and a half to two hours at most. A party can start at

11:30, include sandwiches, cake and ice cream, or follow nap time, omitting the sandwiches.

2. Keep the party small and invite the mothers to insure that each child has his share of attention, supervision and fun.

3. Plan lots of individual activities, because give-and-take manners do not usually develop until nursery-school days.

—Toys and more toys

—Balloons to sit on and try to pop

—Fingerpainting while wrapped in old sheets or plastic—in the garage or out of doors.

4. Avoid needless concern by removing breakables and hazards.

5. Children have fun exploring an enclosed play yard, weather permitting.

6. After refreshments, provide prepackaged washcloths.

FIVE TO EIGHT YEARS

By this time children have graduated to the "game set." In general, the five- to eight-year-olds would rather participate than be spectators. Children love to help make a fire and cook their own hot dogs.

1. It is better to run out of time than to run out of games, so plan plenty. In your library or bookstore you can find an enormous number of party ideas.

2. Lots of games mean lots of prizes, and lots of inexpensive prizes mean lots of fun. Remember to have extra prizes for the non-winners—perhaps for "best sport" or "biggest helper."

3. Let children decorate a sheet with waterproof marking pens. On the party day it doubles as a tablecloth and later becomes a child's favorite sheet.

4. Supply icings and trimmings and let youngsters decorate cupcakes which they devour on the spot or take home.

5. A memorable favor: a Polaroid photo for each child to take home and treasure.

6. Other than games:

—Clown or magician

—Pony rides

—Roller or ice skating

—Short train or bus ride

—Playday at the park

—Kite flying, with the kites given as favors

—Picnic at the zoo or beach

—Is a circus in town? Look no further.

—Hayride

—Rented movies or cartoons, available from libraries, are a great calmer-downer toward the end of a party.

If you take children on an outing, keep the group small enough to keep them in tow. For their safety, make a few definite rules including out-of-bounds limits and a central meeting place in case you get separated. Even then, keep your eye on them.

To draw the party to a graceful close, volunteer to take the children home after the festivities. This puts you in the "driver's seat" of the party, too, because you can sense when the children are starting to wind down.

NINE TO TWELVE YEARS

Children of these ages have definite ideas about parties. Parents may make suggestions, but no matter how inspired the suggestions might be, let the children make the final decisions. Surely you remember the stigma attached to "different" food, dress or activities!

1. The misnamed "slumber party" has perennial appeal. It is amazing how much eating, giggling and joking can be crammed into one night.

2. Boys in this age group are fun, funny and *active*. Give serious thought to engaging a high school or college student to take them on a hike, or direct their baseball game or swim.

   We engaged a college student once, but, unfortunately, he was five minutes late. Five minutes was long enough for one little rascal—half boy, half monkey—to shinny himself to the top of the fourteen-foot draperies.

3. Reserve a gymnasium, complete with trampoline and other equipment, and a sports director.

4. Prizes are less important; hearty food more so.

5. Hold back on boy-girl parties until you are sure the youngsters will be comfortable together.

Other Activities

1. Visit a factory, construction site or airport.

2. Kidnap breakfast: alert parents, pick up children in pajamas and robes and take them to a small, out-of-the-way restaurant where you have made reservations and forewarned about the unusual attire.

3. Treasure hunt, either inside or out of the house.

4. Scavenger hunt in the neighborhood.

5. "Message to the Unknown," via helium balloons. Prepare stamped, dated post cards, addressed to each

guest in advance. The message might read, "I am at a birthday party in St. Louis. Please write and tell me where you found this card. Thank you." Then watch the balloons soar, and wait for the answers to trickle in.

INTO THE TEENS

No matter how wonderful parties might be, they take place only periodically. More wonderful is day-to-day hospitality—yours and your children's. For total enjoyment, open your door wide to your teen-agers' friends:

1. Include a friend on a family weekend of camping or skiing, or on a day's outing to the beach.

2. Welcome your children's friends at meal times or for the night.

3. If your teen-agers would like to bring their dates and another couple to dinner, encourage them. Be available but not ever-present.

4. Everyone loves surprises. Children might expect a birthday celebration, but a just-for-fun day can be even more special.

5. Keep the kitchen stocked with simple food for the diet-and-complexion conscious: oranges, apples, celery, carrots, fruit juices, milk, sandwich makings, and cookies made from cereal recipes which go light on the sugar.
   Stock your freezer with hamburgers, casseroles, buns, and bread.

6. Equip your home with sports gear and music for listening and playing.

Moments to remember: Include children in your activities, even if only for a bike ride. Let them know you are there and want them and their friends to be an important part of your lives.

18. MULTIGENERATION PARTIES

A party which includes three or four generations is delightful at the time, and to savor again and again. One immediately thinks of holiday family gatherings, but don't forget those happy just-for-fun days.

Whatever your level on the generation ladder—whether recently married or great-grandparent—you can create a memorable day. It just takes thought.

GENERAL IDEAS

1. Even if you know the stairs are too steep, the weather too warm, or the confusion too great, invite Great-Granny anyway. She will appreciate the invitation and can decide for herself whether to accept.

2. If there are toddlers in the group, consider engaging a high school girl for an hour or two. A sitter can keep the tiny ones occupied, safe and happy.

3. Provide games that many can play. If you are out of touch with the youngsters' current interests, ask their mothers. It is surprising how soon children can play cards and other games that intrigue every age.

4. Young children will be in better spirits if the party hours conform to their normal nap and bedtime schedules. Gather early to visit and play games before an evening meal, then everyone can feel free to leave soon after dinner.

PATIO PARTIES

If you can count on favorable weather, patio parties—buffet or barbecue—are ideal for multiages, and simplify the hostess's work.

1. Children are content to sit any place, but many adults are more comfortable at tables or with lap trays. Try to arrange seating in both sun and shade.

2. Gather together balls, frisbees, and games many enjoy, such as horseshoes or croquet.

3. If you barbecue, be happy that everyone, from children to octogenarians, likes hamburgers, hot dogs or shish kabobs.

4. For a cold lunch, serve meats, sandwiches and salads. Don't waste your time preparing fancy chicken sandwiches for children—invariably they look for peanut butter.

   For dessert—ice cream bars or cups, cookies, and fruit.

AT THE TABLE

Shall the children sit with you or at a separate table? The following ideas might help you decide:

1. When children are treated as adults, they usually absorb the spirit and respond well.

2. A small child will often need help to cut his meat.

3. If you segregate ages, it is difficult to resolve a fair cutoff age. Is Susie a young lady at eleven, while her ten-year-old cousin Tom is banished to the table of children?

4. Let young children take their dessert elsewhere if they get squirmy.

5. Place cards turn a meal into a party.

MENU PLANNING

If it is to be "turkey day," with the traditional holiday accompaniments, don't be surprised if youngsters scorn sweet potatoes and creamed onions in favor of hot rolls and a handful of olives.

After several such frustrations, I decided to serve a buffet assortment to please all ages, tastes and digestions.

WHY I LIKE BUFFET SERVICE

1. Children are more inclined to eat what they choose themselves. An adult can help serve.

2. The hostess-cook can enjoy the day to its fullest because this kind of buffet can be prepared the day before.

MENU FOR INDOOR BUFFET

Depending upon the size of your party, you can choose from the following list or vary with your own preferences and specialties. The entire selection might appear too extensive, but leftovers could provide a delicious variety of lunches and dinners for many days—thanks to refrigerators and freezers.

—Cold corned beef or ham

—Cold meat loaf, shaped skinny and long

—Room-temperature thin-sliced beef

—A creamed chicken or turkey dish, advisable for either end of the age bracket

—Buttered breads or miniature rolls

—Molded aspic salad—easier than last-minute salad assembling

—Relishes or raw vegetables

—Dessert: To please old and young alike, bring out a bowl of ice cream scoops, stored days ahead in the freezer. At serving time, each person creates his own sundae from the assortment of sauces, cubed fresh or barely thawed frozen fruit, whipped cream, nuts, and cherries. For adults, add liqueurs and a small bowl of regular-grind coffee. Coffee? Yes. Pour brandy over vanilla ice cream and sprinkle with coarse ground coffee. It's delicious.

A FAMILY BIRTHDAY PARTY

Birthday parties are generally family affairs. In our family, four of us share March birthdays and pick an agreeable date to celebrate together—four generations of us!

Traditions have become established. One tradition is the unusual sheetcake. Each corner is decorated by one of the children in an individualistic manner, with complete disregard for the colors and style of the other three corners. Result? No Top Award from the Pastry Makers of America, but fun, laughs, and appreciation of their efforts —and anticipation of next March, and the next March, and many Marches together. . . .

19. CHECK LIST FOR A CHAIRMAN

A chairman who plans, coordinates, and produces a large affair is even deeper into entertaining than a hostess who entertains in her own home and is accountable to no one but herself. The following reminders and check lists are for all chairmen who will undoubtedly sprout angel wings for agreeing to take charge.

TEAS

The chapter on teas, page 73, includes everything one must do. The chairman must separate the different jobs and assign each to a person or committee to carry through. The following is a workable breakdown by committees and duties:

1. Invitations. Decide where to send responses. It helps guests if the location of the tea and the response address are the same.

   If you plan to include the press, attach a personal note to the written invitation or ask one of the members to follow up with a telephone call.

2. Name tags. If desired, write in large letters with a broad or felt-tipped pen. Members' tags can be prepared ahead and arranged alphabetically.

3. Tea table and appointments, including tea and coffee services.

4. Tea sandwiches. The chairman should not leave too much to chance. She will regret saying, "Please bring four dozen open-faced sandwiches," only to find plate after plate of colorless cream cheese sandwiches. Instead, she can ask what kind each committee member

would like to bring, and suggest varieties to make up a representative assortment.

5. Cookies or cakes.

6. Candy and nuts—a good chairman designates amounts and kinds.

7. Napkins—specify number and color or theme.

8. Punch table, if planned. Bowl, cups and non-syrupy punch.

9. China and silver to borrow or rent.

10. Decorations.

11. Parking and traffic. This might entail hiring parking attendants, police, or shuttle buses from a central parking area.

12. Pouring chairman assigns pourers and alerts them when it is time to change shifts. She must also be prepared to find instant replacements.

13. Hostess chairman appoints other hostesses to help her.

14. Kitchen chairman appoints helpers to make tea and coffee, arrange sandwiches and cookies, replenish the tea table and remove plates.

15. Clean-up committee. This should be separate from the kitchen committee.

16. One person should be responsible for marking dishes and other possessions and returning them.

COFFEES

If your club membership is small, consider giving an informal coffee instead of a formal tea. Each member can take part, but duties will be less demanding. Members will then be free to concentrate on hospitality, which, after all, is the main purpose.

A modified plan can be drawn from the coffee party described in chapter 7. The menu, if simplified, will minimize kitchen and clean-up work.

COCKTAIL PARTIES

Many of the same committees listed for the tea chairman are needed for a cocktail party. Check to see which apply, and also refer to chapter 12 for additional supplies and suggestions.

1. Except for very large benefit affairs which require professional bartenders, husbands and dates are usually drafted into service.

2. Drinks can be supplied by the hosts or from the club's treasury or members can buy their own drinks to cover costs.

3. A thoughtful gesture: a gift of flowers or a plant to the hosts who give their home for the evening.

HOUSE TOUR, GARDEN TOUR OR BAZAAR

Garden and house tours are excellent fund raisers. To attract ticket buyers, the homes or gardens selected are usually beautiful, large or unusual.

If, in your area, no homes come into these classifications, don't despair. A novel idea is a tour of added-onto homes, some by do-it-yourselfers, others by contractors. Imaginative, practical ideas within everyone's potential are quite an attraction.

Another variation is a progressive food-tasting luncheon —one course at each home—and a glimpse of the house and garden.

The chairman can delegate these duties:

1. If refreshments will be served (customarily they are), check the tea chairman's list in this chapter and use whatever applies to your plan.

At affairs of this kind, tea is an added feature, not the main attraction, therefore the menu can be considerably simplified and chairman duties combined.

2. Procuring homes. When requesting the use of homes, explain whether the tour will be by invitation or open to the public. It is better to have a refusal now than dissatisfaction later. Also explain that it is not necessary to open every room. Some rooms can be roped off and viewed from the doorway; bedrooms are often completely out of bounds.

3. The invitation committee is in charge of ticket sales and turning over the proceeds to the club treasurer.

4. Publicity chairman. If you wish publicity, choose a chairman who has a good relationship with the press.

5. Traffic and parking chairman. Instead of serving tea, some tours arrange lunch at a club or restaurant with ample parking space. From there, minibuses or private cars driven by volunteers transport guests in comfort.

6. Hostess chairman should station a hostess in each room open for viewing. Guests might be offended if it appeared hostesses were "on guard." To dispel this thought, hostesses greet guests, chat with them, and point out an interesting feature of the room.

    Sometimes a ladies specialty shop will arrange a fashion show by co-ordinating the hostess-model's gown with the décor.

7. Provide plastic or canvas runners for high-traffic areas and install them securely to prevent accidents.

8. Reminder: See that your organization is adequately covered by insurance.

9. Near the entrance, place a prominent "No Smoking" sign and a container, partially filled with sand, for cigarette disposal.

10. Flower-arranging committee. Select a chairman who is both tactful and talented. The chairman should consult with the home lender and try to provide flower arrangements that will please them both.

FUND-RAISING TOURNAMENTS

Backgammon, domino and bridge tournaments are perennial favorites, and therefore almost always financially successful for the organization and fun for the participants.

They can be held in one location, such as a hotel, club or rented room, or divided into as many private homes as needed. Some people prefer the larger, single location where they can see and be seen; others enjoy the atmosphere of a home party. Both methods have merits.

A hot or cold lunch can be prepared by members (except of course in a club or hotel), catered or ordered. Lunches served in decorative baskets or boxes are a boon to the clean-up committee.

Although the object of a volunteer fund-raising event is to make as much profit as possible, the club should not stint on hiring a *professional director*. Play will be immeasurably smoother and the day happier with an impersonal director in charge.

If play takes place simultaneously in several homes, the director takes up headquarters in one home. There he or she can be reached by telephone to post scores and settle problems if they occur.

Every competition does not have to relate to games around a table. You can also organize a more active tournament—golf, tennis, Ping-pong or almost any game or sport.

. . . And Still More

A good chairman thinks of every detail, delegates responsibilities, then double checks to be certain none of her committee members have run into a snag.

Having done all that, one might think she has nothing more to do but admire how well the cogs mesh.

Not so! The day of the event, she must keep alert to everything so she can quickly, and quietly, fill in wherever she is needed.

That isn't all! There remains the accounting and a review. Her written report can be valuable to future chairmen.

Finally: thank-you notes to everyone who contributed. Now we understand why a hostess who knows how to organize is a good chairman, and why a good chairman is a superhostess.

20. CLUB OR CIVIC EVENTS IN YOUR HOME

If yours is the conveniently accessible house with adequate parking and a large living room, you can be certain your name will head the list—the list of home lenders. Requests will come from several sources—volunteer organizations, clubs you belong to and those you don't, political candidates, and civic groups.

In your desire to co-operate, don't let yourself give a hasty, impulsive "yes." Take time to decide, because once you consent, you are *honor bound to carry through*—except in the most dire emergency.

If you have questions, consult the general chairman; she is the only one who can explain the complete plan. Ask her what your responsibilities would be, and find out if the event is fund-raising or social, open to the public, by invitation, or limited to club members.

When you decide to lend your home, do it cheerfully. Except for getting your home ready, you needn't be deeply involved. The chairman will attend to the details (chapter 19).

Following are some typical home-lending occasions:

TO INTRODUCE A POLITICAL CANDIDATE
OR DISCUSS A CIVIC ISSUE

Meetings are held as morning coffees for ladies, or in the evenings so both men and women can attend. Unlike a purely social gathering, people attend because of a common interest.

1. Even if someone else organizes and sponsors the event, hosts should make guests feel welcome. People you don't know, or whose names you can't remember, will

come. Shake hands and introduce yourself by your first name—"I am Barbara Follett," *not Mrs.* Follett.

2. If you cannot leave the door to make further introductions, point out the candidate, speaker or chairman and encourage guests to introduce themselves.

3. Hosts usually provide nothing more than coffee and coffee cake in the morning, coffee and cookies in the evening. A friend can help by directing guests toward the refreshment table, and seeing that it is kept supplied.

4. If a speaker presents a controversial subject, no matter how you feel about the issue, remember you are still the hostess. Let the listeners weigh the facts and draw their own conclusions. Just be available to say goodbye and let them know you appreciated their coming.

A CLUB EVENT, SOCIAL OR FUND RAISING

Many working volunteer organizations treat themselves to a once-a-year tea, coffee, cocktail party or barbecue. The purpose may be to introduce prospective members, display their achievements, or simply to entertain themselves and their friends.

If the event is to take place in your home, pray for an efficient chairman patterned after the ideal chairman outlined in the previous chapter. No matter what she decides, let *her* take charge. It might not be easy for you to keep a hands-off attitude, but there is never room for two chairmen.

Behind the scenes, you can:

1. Unclutter your refrigerator to make room for the members' offerings.

2. Provide an outdoor mat and a place for umbrellas and raincoats.

3. Stock a few reserve supplies, such as coffee, lemons and soda—just in case.

4. Unless you or the club members engage kitchen help, count on helping the clean-up committee. It is difficult for others to know where things belong in an unfamiliar kitchen.

5. You will probably do your own flower arranging for a club event where the emphasis is on guests and sociability. However, if the house itself is featured, such as a house tour, a flower-decorating chairman will either assist you or take over completely.

We always think of hospitality as sharing our home with friends. You won't regret having extended the boundaries to include your friends' friends.

21. TANDEM PARTIES

Many hosts get into the swing of party-giving and give a series, perhaps a few weeks apart. Others of us go a step further and occasionally plan parties on consecutive days or evenings.

Don't let the idea of tandem parties frighten you. All you need is an extra spurt of energy; the rest is easy, provided the two parties are exactly the same.

Right down the line, everything you do for the first party takes care of the second one automatically—all of which saves time, effort and expense. Let us consider some of the advantages:

1. Buy twice as much in one marketing spree.

2. Prepare double amounts before the first party.

3. Flower arrangements serve double duty.

4. A flick of the dustcloth should take care of the second-day house cleaning.

5. Silver won't need another polishing.

6. Your china, crystal and serving pieces will be assembled and ready to use again.

7. One order of party equipment held over for an extra day is less costly than two separate deliveries.

8. Help will need less preparation time the second day. Less time means less expense.

9. If parties exhilarate you, you will be ready for double the fun.

Now, check these warnings:

1. If party-giving leaves you limp, you might be too exhausted to enjoy a second one so soon.

2. If friends are apt to compare notes, you had better mention that you are having two parties. Otherwise, one guest might convince another that the date is for Saturday, not Friday.

3. To keep comparisons favorable, make both parties identical.

4. Have two sets of linen available, even if you have to borrow. Washing and ironing on the second day would break the party spell.

When a special occasion comes along, try a two-day celebration. If one party is fun, two is *more* fun. But not three! I tried three—that was one too many.

22. GIVING A PARTY IN ANOTHER'S HOME

It could happen and probably will: Sometime you will give a party in someone else's home. You might cohost, help a friend or relative, or plan a birthday or housewarming surprise.

All these occasions can be as pleasant as when entertaining alone at home, but each is a challenge that causes one to rearrange and enlarge her thinking. This chapter includes plans for two parties—joint hostessing and a surprise party.

JOINT HOSTESSING

Two friends often find it convenient and fun to give a party together. The old cliché, "Two heads are better than one," can well apply to joint-hostessing. One thought inspires another until soon the ideas pop back and forth like Ping-pong balls.

A party with two hostesses takes more than average planning. When entertaining alone you can make flash decisions and change your mind every few minutes. Not so with a joint party. Each hostess can offer ideas, but decisions have to be agreeable to them both.

When the party is in the other person's home, let her be chairman of the board and—no matter how capable you are—demote yourself to vice-chairman.

As you know, the major work takes place behind the scenes in the home where the party is held. Nothing you do will be too much to compensate, so take over everything you can think of:

1. Do the running-around errands—marketing and borrowing.

2. Write and mail the invitations.

3. If you are to share cooking, use your own kitchen as much as you can.

4. Offer to help arrange flowers or at least supply them.

5. After the party, stay until everything is finished. "Everything" includes:

   —Washing glasses and ash trays.

   —Leaving everything perfect.

   —Assuming the responsibility of returning borrowed or rented items.

6. Someone has to wash the table linens. A gold star on your forehead if you do them.

7. Two hostesses or two couples—the same principles of helpfulness and co-operation apply. The only difference is twice as much fun.

If you end by feeling you've done more than your share, that's a *good* feeling.

A SURPRISE PARTY

A surprise party that really surprises is a great satisfaction, and worth all the conniving. Most fun are the devious plots, subterfuges and teamwork, but there is usually one unknown factor to contend with—the human element.

The human element was the problem my husband ran into when he planned a surprise dinner party for me. Every moment of my day was supposedly accounted for, as I was scheduled to move through a succession of engagements, always accompanied by a companion-spy. I was to be passed from friend to friend somewhat like the baton in a relay race.

What could go wrong with such a carefully charted

plan? *I could.* I simply did not co-operate. I was determined to drop in at home between engagements to look through the mail, change my dress or check on the children and no persuasion could stop me. I learned afterward that each stop at home meant hastily swooping the preparations into closets, an unused bedroom, and once into the empty washing machine.

That evening I was completely astonished—after all, I'd been home off and on all day and seen nothing suspicious!

A surprise party in another's home is not easy when one doesn't know where they keep their equipment, or even what equipment they have. When we planned a housewarming we decided that, in addition to food and drink, we had better provide other essentials. Our check list included:

—Extra glasses and some large serving dishes

—Ice brought in ice buckets

—Flowers, prearranged in containers

—Chafing dishes and fuel

—Extension cord for coffee maker and heating equipment

—Tablecloth, candles, cocktail napkins

Giving the party at home with familiar equipment would have been far easier, but not nearly the fun. We loved seeing that the honorees were literally guests in their new home.

Try a surprise party sometime. Besides the fun, it is a short course in precise and complete planning.

23. PARTY DECORATING

Decorations set the mood of a party. Is yours to be formal, casual, simply elegant or elegantly simple?

A colorful table set with checked gingham, flowers or fruit in baskets, colorful pottery and glasses, pewter and colored-handled flatware instantly conveys an informal, charming country look, suitable for a summer lunch or Sunday supper.

At the other end of the scale, one glance at a table set with an elaborate lace cloth, tall branched candelabra, cut-glass goblets and a centerpiece arranged in an epergne of crystal and silver confirms that the affair is traditional and rather formal.

The use of color does not necessarily imply informality. Another table might be even more colorful than the ginghamed one but, because of the fine quality of its appointments, convey a look of elegance: a cover of rich Thai silk, brocade or a fine obi; graceful stemmed crystal; Royal Crown Derby plates in brilliant emerald, royal blue, vermilion and shining gold. Colorful but elegant!

TABLE-DECORATING IDEAS

1. A centerpiece at a sit-down dinner should not obstruct vision across the table. It is disconcerting to hear a voice emerge from the flowers or to see heads peer around them. Keep the arrangement below eye level, or raise it above.

2. The most familiar below eye-level arrangement is the long, low symmetrical shape.

Seat yourself while you make this arrangement because that is how your guests will view it.

3. Dramatic, above eye-level arrangements are less familiar.

4. Bring flowers above eye level by suspending a container from the ceiling or light fixture. A hanging container can go formal or informal depending on style of arranging, and the material of the container itself. Invisible plastic cord or a suitable chain is strong enough to bear the weight.

5. Other considerations, regardless of tradition or fashion:

   —The shape of the table. A round arrangement for a round table. An oval container for either an oval or rectangular table.

   —The size and scale of the room. A gigantic arrangement in a small dinette would be as incongruous as a little fistful of forget-me-nots in a banquet hall.

6. Flickering candles at eye level are bothersome to anyone wearing glasses. Light cast upward is soft and flattering and women love it.

   Attractive little glass candleholders are available to hold two-inch candles. They can be arranged in a num-

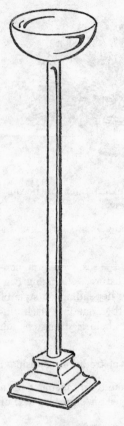

The tall container in the diagram is effective used singly or in pairs. Its material dictates its effect: more formal if silver or crystal, informal if brass, bronze or carved wood. It can be improvised by assembling a bowl on top of a tall candlestick, approximately 27 inches overall. The flowers will add another 6 or 8 inches. The base of the support must be heavy so it won't topple.

ber of ways to make them more important-looking: encircling an arrangement; a single candle at each place setting; at intervals down the table; in clusters.

Keep all candles at a safe distance from arrangements containing flammable materials, or direct the heat away by using glass hurricane chimneys.

7. There is a trend toward the bare-table look. Instead of a cloth or standard-sized place mats, one can protect the table top with linen, lace or crocheted doilies small

enough not to show from beneath the plates. This style of setting does not conflict with the centerpiece, rather, it allows one to feature it.

8. No rule requires center-of-table arrangements. Vary them as you please:

—Space several small containers the length of the table.

—Place arrangements at opposite corners.

—Push one end of the table against a wall or window if you don't need that space for seating. Try a high, spectacular arrangement at the blank end.

9. For buffet tables:

—If the table is against a window or wall, a tall arrangement looks well. Place it to the back so guests won't have to reach across or around it.

—If the table is freestanding for guests to walk around, a center arrangement is best. Make it as high or low as you like.

—An expert artist-arranger created a decoration so tall that he incorporated the flowers into the chandelier centered above the table. The flowers flowed into its curves. If I tried such a daring arrangement, it might be grotesque; his was spectacular and beautiful.

—Try a decorated Christmas tree, the size of a chandelier, suspended upside down from the ceiling.

QUICK, EASY OR INEXPENSIVE IDEAS

Flowers are not always easy to obtain. Even when they are available, one might not have time or the ability to arrange them successfully. What are some alternatives?

1. Art objects, such as porcelain figures or sculpture.

2. Shells or glorious hunks of crystal, coral or colored quartz on a low stand, tray, mirror or complementary fabric.

3. Arrangements of grapes, other fruits or vegetables. Ivy leaves substitute well for grape leaves and are considered non-toxic.

4. House plants.

5. Outdoor potted plants ready to whisk into the house for brief visits. Many varieties of potted plants are suitable for your table if the color is attractive and they are cleanly shaped:

   —Cyclamen

   —Succulents

   —Fibrous begonias and the newer Reiger begonia

   —Azaleas

   —Herbs, they are fragrant, too.

   —Ferns

   —Boxwood

   —Miniature ivy

   —Miniature bonzai trees

   Ivy, boxwood and succulents are important in their own right, but they can also be embellished to co-ordinate with your table for a holiday season. Enrich these with small ornaments, or fruit, such as miniature pomegranates or limes. Impale one end of the fruit on a wooden skewer and stick the other end into the pot.

6. Greenery. Pine or camellia foliage lasts particularly well. One can add a few flowers or even a single flower or art object for color accent.

7. Inexpensive flowering plants are becoming increasingly available. Enjoy a chrysanthemum plant as long as it is

fresh. As it begins to fade, cut the remaining blooms to use as a colorful accent in an arrangement of greens.

8. Let your imagination and inventiveness run rampant. Take your inspiration from anything you admire— weeds, a picture, fabric, fruit, art object, or a foreign country perhaps with a co-ordinated menu.

 —Not everything unusual is pleasing, but if an idea intrigues you, try it. Your own eye and reaction will usually tell you if you were successful.

 —Consider special themes, such as a going-away party, baby shower, sports event, or a holiday. Each theme suggests ideas or colors.

WE DINE WITH OUR SENSES

What we hear, touch, see and smell adds to or detracts from our fifth sense—taste.

1. Hearing

 —Choose music appropriate to the mood or theme you want to carry out.

 —Happy voices and laughter increase the noise level, but those sounds are expected and welcome; make every effort to reduce the level of irritating sounds.

 —When acoustics are poor and sounds reverberate, one might consider adding heavier draperies and thicker carpets, or an acoustical ceiling.

2. Touch

 —One notices and takes pleasure in the weight and balance of flatware.

 —Why is wine more pleasing when drunk from a thin crystal goblet than from a thick pottery mug? It must be the sense of touch to the lips.

3. We Eat with the Eye

What could have less eye appeal than boiled white fish, rice and cauliflower served on a white plate?

When harmony of color, arrangement and texture pleases the eye, taste buds respond accordingly. To improve an uninteresting dish, substitute or add something colorful such as:

—A bright red broiled tomato on a bed of watercress

—Pickled beets

—Parboil small, whole summer squash early in the day. Later top with a scoop of frozen spinach soufflé, and bake until soufflé is puffy.

—Fill the centers of large, sautéed mushroom caps with tiny peas and chopped mint.

—For crunchiness and zest, add celery stuffed with chutney.

—Kumquats, lemon wedges dipped in paprika, or limequats. If you like the sharp citrus flavor of limequats, plant the dwarf variety—they are difficult to find in the market.

Think about co-ordinating the menu and décor. That is essentially what we do when we decide that a thorny, but delicious, dark green artichoke does not look well on a delicate rosebud-patterned plate.

I am not advocating that if your room is red and white you must always serve borsch, tomatoes and strawberries; however, it is fun to play with the ideas merely as a game and mental stimulation.

4. Fragrances

No one would question that the sense of smell affects taste. One has only to recall an experience with an unpleasant odor and the accompanying loss of appetite.

Why leave fragrances to chance? Calculate their effect. Then court and magnify pleasant fragrances from plant material, and think of them in relationship to specific foods:

—Citrus with fish.

—Carnation and stock (clove fragrances) with ham.

—Insert mint leaves in your flower arrangement to complement fruit dishes.

—Pungent aromas with curry.

—Geraniums with ground beef.

—Marigolds and zinnias for color and fragrance with gazpacho.

—Violets, gardenias and roses are perfect dessert flowers.

Are you tempted to change the flowers with each course? So am I.

THE REST OF THE HOUSE

So far this chapter has emphasized table decorating, but don't ignore the rest of the house. Even if you have permanent plants—almost as important to decorating as furniture—add a few extra touches.

Exquisite new miniature varieties of chrysanthemums, begonias and cyclamen are the perfect size to place on small tables to enjoy for weeks.

Try for a measure of unity throughout the house, especially in a small home or apartment. Unity does not necessarily mean using one variety of flower everywhere, even though some repetition of feeling is pleasing. One blossom snipped from a plant or important arrangement would not be missed, but would give a special touch to the dressing table or bathroom counter.

WHAT SHALL I WEAR?

The perennial question! Whatever a hostess wears is an integral part of the total effect—as important to the mood as flowers, music, food and setting.

—Color. A woman chooses colors for her home because she reacts happily to them, and they are flattering. It follows that her wardrobe will inevitably include the same colors.

Those who would delve more deeply into the fascinating subject of color psychology can learn *why* they are stimulated by certain colors, calmed by others, and perhaps repelled by still others.

—Effect. A woman can give any impression she chooses by what she wears, and vary it to suit herself or the occasion. At a business dinner when you want your husband to star, choose a somewhat conservative dress and save your glittery look for a holiday party.

Don't let a dress dominate you. How much more flattering to be remembered as a person, not as the lady in orange.

—Poise. Once you are satisfied that you are well-dressed for yourself and the occasion, forget what you are wearing.

—Hosts' fun with clothes.

A hostess may wear hostess pajamas or a long gown even when guests wear short dresses. Some hosts collect colorful jackets or vests to wear at home for a festive look.

A CALL FOR PROFESSIONAL HELP

If for any reason you find it impossible to take care of your own party decorating, you will miss part of the fun. However, rescue is at hand: Most florists and some interior decorators will handle complete table settings and floral decorations for the house. For weddings, they will also decorate the gift-display and cake tables, even to furnishing cloths.

If a florist is commissioned to take charge, he will be able to supply a choice of suitable containers, candelabra, pedestals and other decorative objects to co-ordinate with your own décor.

TIPS

1. Flower arrangements are seldom their best when done under last-minute pressure. Greens and flowers can be picked a day or two ahead. Shake them well to get rid of bugs, harden them in deep water, and keep in a cool place.

2. If you plan to pick flowers from your garden, water the plants thoroughly the evening before and then pick them in the morning when they are fresh and the stems are strong.

3. If a metal container leaks at the base, try this: Dry thoroughly, then pour hot paraffin into it.

4. To avoid spills when adding to your arrangement on an already set table, use a watering can with a long thin spout, or plunge a funnel in the center and pour water through it.

5. You might hope to complete your china set some day. However, remember that a different pattern can be used for each course as long as the feeling is compatible—not delicate china and bold pottery at the same meal.

6. While needle holders are excellent for flower arranging, oasis is easier for those of us who are novice arrangers. Oasis, available at florists, looks like green styrofoam but is extremely absorbent, and can be cut to fit any size container. Soak well before using.

LONGER LIFE FOR CUT FLOWERS

No matter how adept one might be, she will not deny that fixing flowers takes time. Once done, I want mine to last as long as possible.

Some flowers last better if soaked in cold water, others in warm or hot, still others thrive on a shot of vinegar or gin. All flowers last better if the stems are held under water while cutting (use a small bowl) to prevent intake of air.

The following list supplies ways to prolong the lives of many popular varieties of flowers.

LONGER LIFE FOR CUT FLOWERS*

ANEMONE (Japanese): Cut before fully open and condition in cool water up to flower heads.

AZALEA: Cut when three to four florets are completely open. Spray entirely with fine mist of cold water.

BEGONIA: One tablespoon salt to one quart water to condition. Spray flowers of tuberous begonias with fresh water before arranging.

CALLA: Dip ends in alcohol one to two minutes, and be sure to cut stems under water when arranging.

CAMELLIA: Condition (woody material) and quickly submerge leaves in cold fresh water before arranging.

CARNATION: Condition up to flower heads, propping to keep stems straight.

CHRYSANTHEMUM: Split stems if woody. Use three to four tablespoons sugar to each quart water for conditioning. To revive if wilted, place stems in hot water.

COLUMBINE: Rub salt on cut ends—or condition in salt solution.

CYCLAMEN: *Pull* blossoms and leaves from plant, recut, and split stems. Condition overnight.

DAHLIA: Char or dip in boiling water conditioner and in cold water up to flower heads overnight.

DELPHINIUM: Cut when half florets are open. Change water daily.

* Excerpts from a larger list compiled by The Auxiliary to the Society of Crippled Children and Adults of San Mateo County, and recommended by Jack Daniels.

FORSYTHIA: Cut when just beginning to flower, and always cut just below or through a node.

FREESIA: Condition in water up to flower heads, place in room (45–50°) till ready to arrange. Fine-spray branch with cool water when cut.

FUCHSIA: Place stems in boiling water about three minutes, then condition in cold water.

GERBERA (African Daisy): Pick just before full bloom and condition up to flower heads.

GLADIOLUS: Cut in middle of day. Condition (at room temperature) in five tablespoons vinegar to one quart water.

HEATHER: If flower tips wilt, split stems and place in hot water to revive.

HELLEBORE (Christmas Rose): Cut stems to ground and completely submerge in cold water for at least twelve hours.

HYACINTH: Place stem ends in boiling water for one minute.

HYDRANGEA: Cut before fully open. Hold stem ends in boiling vinegar for thirty seconds, or sear ends in flame for fifteen seconds before conditioning.

IRIS: Cut when first flower unfolds. Can't stand sudden changes in temperature.

LARKSPUR: Condition one hour in solution of one-half teaspoon alcohol to two quarts water.

LILAC: Cut when blossoms are partly open. Remove low foliage from branches.

LILY: Remove pollen stamen from flowers before arranging.

MARIGOLD: Remove *all* foliage that would be under water in container. Fresh water daily.

PEONY: Cut when blooms are less than half open and hold stem ends in hot salt water solution five minutes.

PETUNIA: Condition overnight in four teaspoons sugar to one quart water.

PERUVIAN LILY: Cut when half open. Condition in water up to flower heads overnight.

PHLOX: Cut when one fourth to one half open.

POINSETTIA: Char or dip ends in boiling water.

POPPIES: Cut in tight bud and keep in cool dark place (deep water) till ready to arrange.

PRIMROSE: Condition in warm water to start.

RANUNCULA: Cut when three fourths open. Condition in water to flower heads.

ROSE: Pick in bud and remove all lower foliage before conditioning. *Pinch* (do not pull) damaged petals. *Important:* Water in container should be one third of length of stem.

SNAPDRAGON: Cut when about half open. Condition in hot water to start.

SWEET PEA: Condition in eight drops alcohol to one quart water solution.

SWEET WILLIAM: Cut when half open.

SYRINGA: Break stem ends after cutting from bush—scrape and remove as much foliage as possible.

TULIP: Add a little gin to conditioning water (makes them firm and easy to manage).

VIOLET: Submerge in cold water for an hour. Fine mist of cold water helps to keep fresh.

ZINNIA: Cut when fully open. Remove as much foliage as possible. Dip stem tips in boiling water.

24. HOW TO SUCCEED IN ECONOMIZING WITHOUT EVEN SHOWING

I have always contended that the amount of money one spends does not determine the success of entertaining. To quote my book *Check List for a Perfect Wedding*, "The elaborateness or cost of your wedding will not be the factor that will make it outstanding . . . feel free to eliminate expensive frills. . . . But *do not economize on effort and planning* the essentials that will make your wedding beautiful, and add to your guests' enjoyment and comfort." These views are more than a theory; I have also helped friends plan outstandingly beautiful receptions "on a shoestring."

With all entertaining, think of hospitality and your pleasure in sharing, then offer whatever you have with pride and satisfaction.

Almost everyone economizes to one degree or another, so take heart. Instead of calling it budgeting, which could imply scrimping, think of it as wise home-and-money management. It needn't be obvious.

Consider some of the many forms of entertaining listed in this book. A lunch, brunch, afternoon or evening party might cost less than a dinner party, and be equally pleasant; however, there is no need to exclude dinners from your life style.

The following ideas save $'s and ¢'s without showing:

One Big Don't
Don't skimp on quantity. If you end up with leftovers, call that good management. From one shopping trip and one cooking spree, your meals will be prepared for later in the week, or ready to freeze for future use; they will not be wasted.

Do's

Let us discuss dinners, although the same principles will apply to any form of entertaining you choose.

1. Study the profusion of cookbooks and women's magazines, and start collecting delicious, low-cost recipes. You will find your ideas and cooking capabilities expanding.

   It is not what you cook, but how imaginatively you cook it, that will make the impression. If you previously considered stew ordinary family fare, transform it to boeuf Bourguignon, ragout, or lamb Navarin Printanier (spring vegetables) by adding the appropriate wine and herbs that will make it worthy of entrées listed on menus of the world's finest restaurants. Remember delectable baked casseroles or inexpensive fish in season with an elegant sauce marguery, Mornay or véronique.

   If you like beef, bypass the budget-killing filet roast and ask your butcher about the first three inches of top round—a cut variously named in different areas of the country. Whether you call it London broil or something else, it is equally tasty hot or at room temperature and sliced very thin at a forty-five-degree angle.

2. American cooking often falls into a pattern of generous portions of meat, a starch and a vegetable.

   In many foreign countries where meat is scarce or expensive, it is used sparingly but in an inspired manner. We know how far one pound of ground beef will stretch when making spaghetti or lasagna.

   Search for other ethnic dishes which conserve meat, but add seasoning and imagination. Look to Mexico, Greece, Italy, Scandinavia, the Far East, India and France. These countries and others are masters at incorporating pasta, rice, beans, pancakes, breads or potatoes with meat, fish or poultry into delicious and economical dishes.

3. Discover homemade soups thick with meat, chicken or vegetables. If one accumulates and freezes otherwise unusable leftover bones, there is little more to add for a rich soup stock.

   Soups alone can comprise a complete dinner, as proven by a hostess who invited friends for an evening of "Soup and Games." She was overly generous with her four delicious homemade varieties: beef and vegetable, cream of mushroom, chicken and barley, and Senegalese with its touch of curry. With warmed bread and pie, it was a feast.

   Even one hearty, meal-in-itself soup, such as minestrone or fish chowder, would have sufficed.

4. Keep an open mind when you go to the market, and look for seasonal "specials." To duplicate a summer menu in winter could be quite costly.

5. By following well-publicized fuel-saving tips, such as complete oven dinners, you will save money, as well as kilowatts.

6. List everything you need well in advance. Your list will benefit you in several ways:

   —You will have time to take advantage of specials whenever and wherever they are advertised.

   —Stagger your buying over a longer period of time. Just as some efficient household managers buy Christmas gifts throughout the year to avoid the crunch of January bills, you can dilute the drain on your budget by spreading out the cost of a party.

   Examples: drinks and mixes, foods you can freeze, canned and packaged goods, candles and paper goods.

   —Convenience food is often more expensive than home-prepared. For example, grate your own cheese, a pound or two at a time, and store it tightly covered in your freezer.

—To avoid impulse buying, never shop when you are hungry.

7. Listing errands by the route you travel saves backtracking and extra trips, therefore it saves transportation expenses as well as time.

8. Be overly generous with predinner snacks, especially if they include a colorful, large plate of raw vegetables served with a well-seasoned dip.

   At the end of this chapter, you will find nine excellent ways to use mixed vegetables. After you read the recipes, you will see why you can afford to be generous.

9. Splurge on one little unnecessary luxury just for fun. For example, one of the following:

   —Garnish the meat with mushrooms, either broiled or easily baked in the oven.*

   —Add a few stalks of crisp, uncooked asparagus to the vegetable platter you serve before dinner. A gourmet treat.

   —Place one perfect, luscious, red strawberry on top of a simple, individual dessert serving.

10. The most expensive wines are not always the most pleasing. Have your own private wine-tasting sessions in advance, then choose the one that fits your personal taste as well as your pocketbook. It is better to have enough of an acceptable brand than a stingy amount of expensive wine.

11. Unless garden flowers are readily available, you will find ideas for inexpensive, attractive decorating in chapter 23. First choice might be a fruit or vegetable centerpiece to eat for the balance of the week.

12. You needn't sacrifice the beauty of candles. Candle factories sell their "seconds" (only slightly irregular) at

a considerable discount. Try to locate an outlet in your area.

13. To get around the high cost of firewood, one can make logs out of rolled newspapers. The moment they char they look like wood. Some people make the consistency more woodlike by soaking them in water and drying in the sun; however, they also burn well without being treated.

14. Even if your circumstances are limited—and remember, *everyone has a limit*—there is no excuse for an uncared-for look.

   —Give your flatware an extra buffing.

   —Check table linens ahead of time and iron them with care.

   —If your linens have become shabby, don't use them. Either buy new ones, or create something artistic from the enormous variety of inexpensive but effective materials available at your fabric shop or hobby store.

   —Follow the bare-table fashion (page 142, item 7).

A guest would feel uncomfortable if he sensed that you strained your budget for him, so don't be trapped into mentioning the price of anything in your home—bargain or extravagance. Without reminders, everyone is aware of inflation.

To keep economizing from showing is a challenging game, and everyone likes both a challenge and a game.

RECIPES

HOW TO USE LEFTOVER VEGETABLES

1. Baked, mixed vegetables are delicious and pretty.
   Slice and arrange any combination of raw vegetables you have on hand in a buttered, flat baking dish. Top with a few

dabs of butter and a sprinkling of seasoning. Seal the baking dish with foil. Don't add water; the moisture in the vegetables is sufficient. Bake in a medium oven about 20 minutes if you like them crisp.

Even though various vegetables normally require different cooking times, for some unfathomable reason they cook well this vitamin-retaining way. After you experiment a time or two, you will learn what size slices are best.

2. Tossed mixed salad.

3. Chilled gazpacho soup, Spain's national dish, is our favorite. On a thirty-day visit to Spain, we ate gazpacho soup sixty times—never twice the same. I say "ate" instead of "drank" because it is thick.

There are as many recipes for this soup as cooks in the kitchen, so feel free to experiment and free-wheel. Basically, gazpacho consists of fresh tomatoes—the riper the better.

EASY BLENDER GAZPACHO

Blend until liquid:

2 pounds (906 gms.) cored, unpeeled tomatoes
Small piece green pepper
3 slices peeled cucumber
3 tablespoons (45 ml.) olive oil
2 tablespoons (30 ml.) vinegar (we like ½ red wine and ½ cider)
Salt and pepper
(Authentic gazpacho calls for garlic—we don't use it.)

Strain. Add crumbs made from two slices of French or white bread. Also a little cold water, tomato juice or bouillon. Blend well. Taste for seasoning. Refrigerate. Must be cold!

Dice: 1 peeled, seeded tomato, remaining green pepper and cucumber, small onion, hard-cooked egg. Either mix diced vegetables into soup and top with croutons, or serve them in condiment dishes.

Think a moment: The ingredients of gazpacho and a tossed salad are almost identical, even to the oil and vinegar. If you are a purist, chop or purée the vegetables from a leftover salad bowl; if you are more daring, purée the lettuce too for your own version of cold soup.

4. Niçoise Salad. As served in France, the recipe is precise; however, as with gazpacho, feel free to improvise and use other vegetables.

NIÇOISE SALAD

Tear lettuce in bite-sized pieces and arrange the following on top: tomato wedges, cooked string beans, and dollar-sized slices of boiled potatoes. Mound tuna in the center. Garnish with pitted black olives and quartered hard-cooked eggs. Top with anchovies and capers.

Toss with a dressing of olive oil, red wine vinegar, Dijon mustard, salt and pepper.

5. Add to soup: Cut leftover vegetables smaller and make vegetable soup. Or add chopped vegetables to whatever homemade or canned soup you already have on hand.

6. Cream soup: Boil a few potatoes, onion, celery and seasonings in chicken broth. Purée in your blender with one or more taste-compatible vegetables.

7. If there is a baby in the household, cook and purée whichever varieties are on his diet.

8. Warmed cherry tomatoes, seasoned with olive oil, fresh sweet basil, salt and pepper are an elegant meat accompaniment. Just swish them around to coat completely, warm briefly, and remove from the oven before the skins pop.

9. Leftover sliced mushrooms. Mound in center of buttered foil. Dot with more butter and sprinkle with a teaspoon or more of powdered-beef-stock base. Fold into a package and pierce once or twice. Bake in a moderate oven about 20 minutes.

Don't you often wish your fairy godmother would whisk the used dishes from the table, wash them clean and shiny, and replace them in their cabinets? If you keep wishing, maybe *yours* will; mine never has.

As long as it must be done, don't fight it. Do it as quickly as you can.

No single cleaning method satisfies everyone, primarily because, as I see it, cleaner-uppers fall into three classifications:

1. *The compulsive type* who can never relax until the kitchen is completely clean. Compulsive cleaners have been known to leave guests waiting in the living room while they do the dishes.

2. *The take-it-in-stride type.* Many couples enjoy doing the dishes together after the guests leave. They use clean-up time to compare party notes, repeat little anecdotes, and unwind.

3. *The ignore-it-until-morning type.* One lovely hostess, and gourmet cook besides, says she enjoys her guests so much that the thought of washing a dish that same night would dispel her state of euphoria.

No matter which type you are at heart, the following ideas might suggest a slight compromise that won't go against your nature.

Substitute for an Electric Dishwasher

The following equipment is guaranteed for life with no mechanism to get out of order:

Just before dinner, fill the sink with hot water and dishwashing detergent. When you bring the used dishes to the kitchen, silently scrape off excess food with a rubber spatula, and slip dishes into the bubbly bath to soak.

It makes no difference how long you leave them. Later that evening or the next morning, open the drain, and with a sponge or soft brush, rinse the dishes under hot water as you transfer them to a rack. Air-drying is more sanitary than towel-drying I've heard, and I am delighted to accept the theory.

With a Dishwasher

Manufacturers of most new dishwashers claim that small bits of food left on dishes help to activate detergents. If they say so, why disagree!

Silently swipe off the bones and larger pieces of food, and you can slip dishes into the slots as quickly as stacking them on the counter.

Cleaning the dishes as you take them out to the kitchen is not feasible for more than six. If attending to dishes would hold up dessert, fill the sink with water and slip dishes in for a long soak. When you get around to transferring them to the dishwasher, food will not have hardened.

Let the dishwasher work for you. If it won't hold everything at one time, don't hand wash the surplus—put it aside for the next load.

A hostess who appears to be working too hard makes guests feel uncomfortable. Try to do your clean-up behind the scenes. Here are a few basic reminders:

1. Wash utensils you've used for preparation, so the kitchen is clear before dinner starts.

2. Soak pots and pans in soapy water before announcing dinner.

3. The sounds of running water and scraping dishes advertise too noisily that you are cleaning up and make your guests feel they should offer to help. Either leave the dishes or scrape off excess food the silent way—with a rubber spatula.

4. Set a bowl of hot soapy water in the corner of your sink and place silverware into it immediately.

5. Every guest will understand if you slip away for a moment to put perishables in the refrigerator. But stop there; you can reorganize the food the next day.

6. Three important jobs after guests leave:

> First: Bank the fire so that burning logs cannot roll out.
>
> Second: Gather ash trays into one safe place.
>
> Third: Submerge napkins in a basin of water with a pre-wash solution. Spots will either come out or be easier to treat, after an overnight of soaking. Exception: rub wet salt and water on a red-wine spot and let it stand for twenty-four hours.

7. At your leisure, polish silver hollow ware and wrap it securely in *airtight* plastic wrap. It can stay untarnished for years! Remember that rubber bands and silver are enemies; keep them apart.

To me, kitchen clean-up is the least interesting of all household chores, probably because it is so repetitious. But like it or not, there it is—not to brood over, but to finish as quickly and painlessly as possible.

A friend and I were bemoaning the time we wasted in the kitchen. Since we were both enrolled in an exercise class, we improvised a set of exercises to do while working in the kitchen. We called it our "Kitchen Ballet."

1. At the sink, instead of hunching your shoulders tensely, drop them, and consciously take slow, deep breaths.

2. Rise up and down on your toes—pointed out, then pointed in; that exercise is good for muscles and balance.

3. Strengthen feet, legs and posture by walking from stove to sink, sink to refrigerator on tiptoes. Stretch your arms high.

4. When putting dishes in the cupboard, stand at right angles to it, more than an arm's length away, and s-t-r-e-t-c-h until you feel the pull in your waistline and abdomen. Stop, and turn to stretch the other side.

This list could go on and on. Originate your own stretchers and benders. Suddenly, time in the kitchen is productive and fun.

26. IF YOU NEED EXTRA HELP

If you need assistance for a large or ambitious party, you will ask these questions:

1. How can I find someone to help?

2. What will I have to pay?

3. What should I expect from someone I engage?

The answers will depend upon a number of factors, so let us discuss them one by one.

HOW CAN I FIND SOMEONE TO HELP?

1. *From friends*

The list will come primarily from the recommendations of co-operative friends, and can build up over the years.

The unwritten law: One may ask a friend to inquire if her maid has free time or can recommend someone who has. However, one should *not* ask the maid directly; to do so might be considered an encroachment.

2. *Consult your telephone book* if you have no list to fall back on. Look under "Employment Agencies" in the classified section.

When you call an agency, be specific about your requirements. State how many hours you will need a maid and if she is expected to cook. In addition, inquire about references.

Agencies handle references in different ways:

—Some agencies verify references before sending an applicant for an interview.

—Others send bonded help only.

—Some agencies register anyone who applies and leave the checking to the employer. By all means, check references or be willing to risk disappointment at your party.

Discuss rates, keeping in mind they are usually higher than from a personal list because of the fee charged by agencies. The fee is sometimes paid by the client, other times by the employee and included in her rates.

The classified section also lists catering and parking attendant services.

Businesslike parking services need only be told the hour to report and how many cars to expect. Bonded help will take charge at the entrance—a comfort on a dark, rainy or stormy night.

3. *The newspaper* is another source. If the person advertising is available at the time you need her, ask for references.

4. *Make general inquiries.*

5. Don't forget the *placement bureau at local colleges* or other schools. Students often work their way through school by tending bar, parking cars, or doing household work. Some are well qualified.

Teachers, policemen, writers, and many other employed people "moonlight" to turn their extra time into extra cash.

WHAT WILL I HAVE TO PAY?

Rates vary, not only in different parts of the country, but also between cities, suburbs and small towns. Rates also differ by how sought-after and experienced the person is. However, don't be misled into thinking high charges guarantee excellence. Most help will charge the customary rate, regardless of ability.

Rates are figured in various ways:

1. By the hour.

2. On important holidays when demands are great, rates often double or triple.

3. A minimum rate. Five hours' pay is often the minimum for a cook, maid, or butler, three hours for a bartender or parking service, with an hourly rate thereafter.

4. By contract. A caterer is paid a predetermined sum.

By Contract

A catering firm will arrive at the total charge by adding together the following items:

$ ... The cost of each dinner multiplied by the number of guests, known as the "charge per head." *Or*, the total cost of food plus an agreed-upon percentage.

$ ... Charges for the staff's working time.

$ ... Dishes, glasses and other equipment you request.

$ ... Other specified services or provisions, such as music, decorations, drinks, wedding cake.

$$$ Total

At the original consultation, you can roughly estimate the number of guests. The contract will state a cut-off date for specifying a firm number.

Canceling a Contract

If, due to an emergency, you have to call off a party, what is your obligation? A contract is an agreement to pay regardless of personal problems. However, if you cancel far enough ahead, you might be granted some leniency.

Leniency depends upon the caterer's attitude, and often on his relationship with a customer. If you are a good customer, he will probably take that into consideration. If it is too late to place the staff elsewhere, you will be fully obligated to pay. If he has not yet purchased the food, he might relieve you of that expense.

Caterers who are also in the restaurant business are often able to use the food, even if you cancel late; if they cannot use it, they will charge you.

Should I Tip?

Tipping is not customary; however, if you are especially pleased and *want* to round off to a higher amount, do so. Don't hesitate to offer surplus goodies to take home; they'll be appreciated. Instead of tipping, send a remembrance at Christmastime to a cook or waitress who has worked for you several times during the year.

How and When Do I Pay?

1. Usually one pays immediately after the party. If help is to leave as soon as the kitchen work is finished, have enough cash on hand, or stash a check and pen in the kitchen.

2. If paying from a bill, mail checks first thing in the morning.

3. A caterer will submit a bill. Again, send his check promptly.

4. If you engage someone to direct parking (a convenience in some areas, a fire-safety law in others), pay him when he reports rather than interrupt the party when he leaves.

WHAT SHOULD I EXPECT FROM SOMEONE I ENGAGE?

First, decide exactly what you want and are willing to pay for and how much you expect to do yourself. Do you want an extra pair of hands? Someone to take over completely? A compromise in between?

Discuss exactly what you have in mind: the number of

guests, menu and type of service. Then inquire if the help can handle the affair comfortably.

From her comments and suggestions, you can modify your plan if need be: perhaps change to an easier type of service (page 23); substitute dishes you can cook in advance; change from broiler hors d'oeuvres which require watching to a less demanding kind; pass appetizers yourself—a gracious and easy way to move from one group to another. Your help might suggest needing another person to assist. If you agree, ask if she can recommend someone she likes to work with.

Classifications of Help

1. *"Mother's helper"* has no reference to age. Under your direction, a mother's helper can assist in many ways— peel, chop, check on something on the stove or in the oven, carry to a buffet table, clear it, and clean the kitchen before and after dinner.

   If a mother's helper returns to your home frequently, bit by bit she can learn your ways, but if she doesn't learn, just be grateful for an extra pair of hands.

2. A *"father's helper"* is what I dub a non-professional bartender—maybe a student or moonlighter.

   Like his counterpart, the mother's helper, he too, is an asset. He relieves the host from active bar duty, and is a boon to a hostess entertaining alone.

   Many young men are extremely competent, however, you or the host should direct him. Set up the bar in advance. Give him a jigger and tell him exactly how you want him to mix drinks. Check every now and then to see that he isn't free-wheeling.

3. A *waitress or butler*

   If you want dinner served with more ease or formality than you can muster by yourself, a waitress or butler is your solution. This means you will have to cook. Plan oven dinners to avoid last-minute top-of-the-stove cooking that requires close watching.

—A waitress will heat hors d'oeuvres and pass them.
If you agree in advance and allow enough time,
perhaps she will help assemble them.

—Occasionally, if a guest list is small, a waitress will
mix and serve drinks. A butler can be counted on
to take care of drinks and direct other help, but not
to make hors d'oeuvres.

—An experienced waitress will know how to serve
correctly, but without a cook in the kitchen, she
will be hard pressed to give proper service unless
you use one of the serving variations (page 23).

—She will clear the glasses and ash trays from the
living room while you eat dessert.

—She will wash the dishes.

—If you have more than six or eight guests, change
to buffet service. One waitress or butler can
remove dishes and serve dessert and coffee. Service
might be slow, but people never mind waiting between courses.

4. *A cook*

—An experienced cook can completely take over the
kitchen, and will do the dishes before leaving.

—Discuss the menu in detail and, together, list the
ingredients you need.

—The cook knows how much preparation time will
be needed. Persuade her to allow plenty of time,
especially if this is her first time in your home.

—A cook is invisible to your guests. You will have to
serve or if you have children perhaps they can
help.

—Post your menu in a conspicuous place. I learned
to write my list in huge letters after seeing a cook
search for reading glasses every time she referred
to my neatly typewritten list.

5. *A cook and a waitress*

This is an ideal combination. Between them they can take over the complete responsibility of a small dinner with no need to improvise. For a larger dinner party, one cook can still prepare it, but you will need additional people to serve.

—It is important for both the cook and waitress to understand the details, so review the menu with them together.

—The preliminaries are yours: setting the table, selecting platters and serving dishes, and having food supplies on hand.

6. *Catered food*

There are services which provide already prepared food. I do not refer to the take-home chow-mein or fried-chicken establishments. Undoubtedly you know about those for quick-and-easy Sunday nights.

In every city and many smaller towns, one can find other types of prepared foods to suit a particular need.

—One company might specialize in tea sandwiches and canapés. What a lifesaver if you have to produce an instant get-together for Aunt Frances' surprise visit!

—Other services range from gourmet casseroles to complete dinners, from pick-up-yourself to delivery in portable ovens. A few telephone calls will acquaint you with what is available, how far ahead of time to order, and prices.

—One type of complete dinner service, although not company fare, can prove invaluable in filling a special need. I refer to daily-delivered, simple meals. This service can assure that a person living alone, or recently home from a hospital, is provided with a hot, balanced daily meal, at a relatively modest cost.

7. *The caterer*

Page 166 explained how caterers operate the financial side of business. Here are more details of what to expect from them.

A professional caterer will provide the food and an adequate staff of cooks, waiters or waitresses and bartenders.

He can supply glasses, dishes, tea service, punch bowls, tablecloths, chairs—almost anything you want.

Some caterers are qualified to handle the decorating as well. If you wish to carry out a theme, they have the experience to co-ordinate food with décor. They will arrange for music, flowers, and other special services you wish. A caterer is responsible for dozens of parties, so have confidence in him and his suggestions.

Caterers prepare much of the food in their own kitchens and transport it in portable ovens. When one's own kitchen facilities limit entertaining to a small group, portable equipment opens vast possibilities.

Even with portable ovens, one might wonder where to seat enormous numbers of guests. Ingenuity and imagination can find ways for All-out Occasions such as the following three:

—Remove most of the household furniture and use floor space freely—dance in the dining room and dine in the living room. Party rental equipment can provide chairs and tables. A moving company will hold your furniture on its van and replace it after the party.

—Set up a tent. We had a tent installed in our parking area for an anniversary dinner-dance. Tables for eight and ten surrounded a portable dance floor.

—If you have a two-car garage, remove bicycles, paint cans and other clutter, and start decorating your temporary party room.

—Keep the floor bare for dancing, or cover it with a borrowed or rented rug.

—One would never guess your tables are planks on sawhorses after pretty cloths cover them.

—Decorate with colorful posters, or to carry out a theme.

—For a summer wedding reception in the country, transform the garage into a garden room by lining its walls with espaliered trees in planter boxes. Reed furniture and an outdoor rug will make the temporary room cool and inviting.

One easily associates the word "catering" with mammoth affairs—wedding and anniversary receptions, debuts and balls. A caterer will also take complete charge of smaller gatherings, such as lunch for sixteen or dinner for twelve.

If you contemplate engaging a certain caterer for the first time, talk to others who have used him unless you have attended parties he handled, or have confidence in his reputation. Recommendations are important. Rarely—but occasionally—one hears of a caterer who underestimated quantity and ran out of food.

8. *Party-givers*

New party-giving services are constantly springing up. Some specialize in children's parties and will furnish everything including decorations, food, entertainment and supervision.

Others are patterned after wedding planners who take complete charge: arranging for all services, caterers, florists, parking attendants; ordering napkins and invitations—even addressing them; co-ordinating before the wedding and supervising from behind the scenes at the reception.

Many party-giving services do not include a culinary department, but will engage a caterer complete with staff for the client. Some party-givers are highly specialized; others are unlimited in what they offer. Some work for a set fee, and others for a percentage of the total bill. In still other cases, the customer will pay no more, but these specialists receive an agent's fee for orders or services they place.

9. *A housekeeper plus one*

If you are fortunate enough to have a permanent housekeeper, let her help decide whom to engage when you need additional help. Two people who work together pleasantly and co-operatively function more efficiently.

Put your housekeeper in charge, with the idea that the extra person is coming to help her.

How grateful we are for the assistance of help when needed for a large party. We can be thankful, too, for all the times we've worked alone. It is only through those experiences we learn how to direct others, and not to expect the impossible.

27. CHILDREN AND PETS AT ADULT PARTIES?

A friend accuses us of having been strict with our children and spoiling our dogs. Guess what—she is right!

I have soul-searched to find why we are so inconsistent, and can fall back on one possible excuse. We feel no responsibility to prepare our dog for future social adjustment out in the world—because we are his world.

It is different with children; one looks toward their future. We wanted ours to learn early that friendships have no age barrier. Consequently, when they joined us briefly at the start of our dinner parties, it became established that our friends were their friends—then and now.

Young children love center stage and are notorious interrupters. Despite this, we worked on the premise that the sooner our children adjusted to adult social ways, the more pleasant it would be for them and us. (I apologize to those child psychologists who advocate that parents adjust to their children's ways.)

As our children became older, they helped us in the early part of the evening when we entertained informally, and they painlessly absorbed the rudiments of hospitality and entertaining to the point where they now surpass us.

When the children were little, as much as we loved them, we didn't want them at our adult parties any more than they wanted Mom and Dad in sleeping bags in the midst of their giggling slumber parties.

As for our dogs, each of them, over the years, has been the most outrageously pampered member of our family. One monstrous afghan slept on the extra twin bed in our daughter's room, where he stretched out happily on his coverlet. What to do when a little chum came to spend the night with our daughter? No problem—just move the dog and coverlet into the guest room.

We are perfect examples of bad examples. Our dog—now a miniature poodle—sits on the sofa even though he nudges a guest's drinking arm. When he kisses the lady who least likes dogs, we are amused. When he steals an hors d'oeuvre, we laugh. He interrupts conversation by bringing the ball for playtime, and if he doesn't interrupt, *we* do—to show off his brilliant tricks!

My husband and I are in complete agreement that dogs should not be imposed on guests. But, just before guests are due, we hurry to brush and comb our poodle to make him presentable for his and our party.

This book now *goes on record* as emphatically advising against annoying guests with one's dog. Dogs should not be the center of attention. They should *not* jump on guests or steal tidbits. You could close him in another room until the party is over. Well, *you* could; *we* couldn't.

We are fond of all animals. It is curious that, among people who profess to love animals, they mean, "all animals except cats." Some people love cats, others tolerate them, still others are repulsed or terrified to be in the same house with them.

A friend who suffers from cat-hair allergy takes this counteraction after being in a home where a cat resides. She sets her clothes dryer to cold air only, and lets it blow through her clothing. In addition to removing hair and lint, minor wrinkles disappear.

As for other little pets your children present for guests to admire—hamsters, rats, turtles, birds, iguanas, or baby crocodiles—remember, even though your children love them and you are used to them, guests might cringe.

Enjoy your children and pets wholeheartedly, but don't expect every friend to share your enthusiasm.

28. A SMATTERING OF DIPLOMATIC AND MILITARY PROTOCOL

You might wonder how necessary are the traditional written and unwritten rules, regulations, conventions and ritual which govern the actions of those required to follow strict protocol.

One will find the rules of protocol are not capricious. Protocol was developed to enable diplomats to function more effectively in their official capacities by avoiding unnecessary irritations, not unlike the help of etiquette in daily social exchange.

Both make for pleasant associations and dealings, and both tend to relieve tensions, misunderstandings and doubts. However, protocol in the diplomatic profession and military life is meant to be followed meticulously, whereas much social etiquette is often only a guideline.

If presently you move in diplomatic or military circles, this chapter is not for you. You will already have learned all you need, or know where to find accurate information and advice.

But it is conceivable that others of us could, at some time, encounter an unfamiliar situation and wish we were better informed.

We need not concern ourselves with entertaining heads of state or other very high-ranking officials and dignitaries, whether of the United States or foreign countries. Their activities are nearly always planned in advance, and the Protocol Office of the Department of State briefs hosts on every detail. In a city such as Washington, D.C., the Protocol Office is always available for advice even as to lesser officials.

But what about foreign visitors or others of official position whose activities are not covered and planned? One might wonder how to address, introduce and seat, as well as about other national and procedural customs. Finding out will undoubtedly put your mind at ease. However, if you are entertaining unofficially at home, don't misplace the emphasis. It would be better to slip up on a formality or two than to cling rigidly to rules while neglecting the warm spirit of hospitality. Your guest should not only recognize but welcome friendly informality.

The following subjects baffle many hostesses. Their discussion is not limited to guests with official positions, but can apply to any visitor including a foreign student.

INFORMATION AND ADVICE

Phone or write the consulate of the visitor's country. The consular staff is prepared and anxious to help you avoid possible embarrassment to yourself or their countrymen. Don't hesitate to ask any questions you are dubious about, no matter how trivial they might seem.

A parallel source of information is headquarters of the nearest Army, Navy or Air Force Command. The Protocol Officer or Flag Lieutenant will brief you fully and accurately on precedence of military personnel and can be helpful in other matters of protocol as well.

CUSTOMS

In general, while being aware and considerate of a foreign visitor's customs, we should maintain those of our own country as long as they will not offend. For example, we all know that in the United States the guest of honor is seated to the right of the host or hostess. Therefore, even if you entertain someone from a country where the designated place of honor is to the left of the hostess (Scandinavian countries) or opposite the host (Japan), you should still seat him to the right of the hostess. If you adjust to his custom, he might misinterpret and feel confused or possibly less honored.

PROMPTNESS

Perhaps your own friends are purposely inclined to arrive late in anticipation of a long cocktail hour. But in diplomatic and military life, the time stated on an invitation is usually taken literally. So, if your doorbell rings promptly at the zero hour, don't be caught without your make-up.

If you switch roles from host to guest, speed up your own arrival time.

If your invitation stated 5:00 until 7:00, don't be surprised if your foreign or military visitor leaves just before 7:00. Most other guests consider they may *arrive* within those hours and leave when they please; but foreign and military guests treat the times on an invitation more seriously.

INVITING

Carry out whichever form you wish—formal, informal or telephoned. A reminder card often follows a telephoned invitation (page 8). Be specific as to dress, time, and whether you are serving a continuous buffet or a seated dinner. If a number of guests will be present, it is sometimes helpful to give your foreign visitor (and perhaps other guests, too) an advance guest list which identifies those who will attend.

TITLE OR DESIGNATION

It is important to know your guest's correct personal title (if any), official position, and comparative rank or precedence. These are too numerous to list, so if the need arises, you had better do your own checking.

Remember: Relative precedence is not nearly so important to us as it is to those diplomats, politicians, and military men who have spent their lives in rank-structured society where it is taken very seriously.

At a social gathering in a private home, it is proper to introduce a non-military man as "Mr. _____, the Consul General of _____(country)_____." If you use a title, it is mandatory to use the correct one. No one appreciates being demoted, even if he knows it is unintentional. For example, we uninitiated might mistakenly think that "Consul" is a short version of the title "Consul General," or that "Counsel" is another way of spelling it. Don't be caught in those mistakes.

In American society, we have considerable freedom of choice when addressing officials. As a general rule one can address an official as "Mr." followed by his rank: Mr. President; Mr. Secretary; Mr. Mayor; Mr. Ambassador. "Your Excellency" is an alternate way of addressing an ambassador. For all designations above that rank, scream for help from the Protocol Office.

Perhaps more important in everyday life is the question at what lower level must one use titles. One is more likely to use them at an official occasion, less likely at a social occasion.

AT MEETING

If you follow the general rule of introducing, giving the woman's name first, you will have no problem. Exceptions would reverse the order if the man were President or a head of state.

The woman makes the first move to shake hands. But if it is to be hand-kissing, the man moves whether or not the lady has offered her hand first.

Hand-kissing in most countries today is more often than not, a gesture left incomplete—merely a move toward a lady's hand. Even the gesture is non-existent in England and most Scandinavian countries.

The question arises—should guests under the same roof introduce themselves to other guests? Yes. In the United States this is expected and customary. Occasionally one might be met by a cold stare. However, that lack of graciousness is the other person's problem, not yours.

DRINKING CUSTOMS

As one finds when traveling, drinking customs vary from country to country. The cocktail hour often tends to be shorter and the drinks lighter—perhaps a wine or apéritif, and in some areas, a non-alcoholic drink is customary for women.

Although as hostess you are not expected to change your own habits, remember that a two-hour cocktail stint could debilitate anyone, especially one who hadn't anticipated such a long delay before the meal.

In many countries, most drinking is done at the dinner table, sometimes with toasts, drinking songs, or other rituals. These can be great fun, particularly if you have taken the time to learn the others' drinking customs beforehand so you feel comfortable rather than confused when you are a guest.

Unless you plan a reasonably brief cocktail period, it is helpful to indicate the dinner hour on your invitations. One can simply state, "Cocktails at 7:30. Dinner at 9:00." Once alerted, guests can time their arrival to suit their own wishes.

To take care of any preference, stock your bar supplies with a wide assortment. An important guest is pleased if the host has gone to the trouble to learn his particular preference and has it on hand.

THE MENU

Certain everyday American fare might be banned in another country. Vegetarians abound; pork is forbidden in some countries, beef in others. The consulate will know if your visitor's diet is restricted. If so, you can avoid serving an unacceptable dish.

Manners of eating vary as much as what is eaten. In the United States, we are taught to eat as silently as possible. Your visitor might have been taught to show his gusto and approval by making appropriate swallows and noises during or after a meal. Before you become critical, realize from his viewpoint he is complimenting you, and your silent ways may indicate to him you do not relish the meal as much.

HOW TO ARRANGE SEATING

At official dinners or lunches strict adherence to precedence or "pecking order" is essential. Every advancement is a step up the ladder, and each individual knows his exact position on that ladder. Wives are sometimes even more acutely aware.

If two men hold the identical rank, the dates they attained them will determine relative precedence. The host's ranking of his guests is nowhere more evident than in table seating. Here, in particular, expert advice from consular, military, or other sources should be sought whenever possible.

At a *non-official* home dinner, your friend with official status may be treated first as a friend—not according to official precedence. One may honor other guests depending upon friendship, age, other distinctions, local situation, or whim. However, it is tactful to let it be known whom you are honoring and why, or that you are following no pattern at all, if that is the case.

An honored guest is seated at the hostess' right and his wife at the host's right.

The traditional host-at-one-end, hostess-at-the-other-end is only one of the ways to arrange a table. The following diagram indicates another plan which creates a center of conversation for the most important guests.

You may also use the ends of the table to create three centers of conversation while honoring two additional guests at the heads.

To share the honors between two couples, see diagram on page 29. Mr. A. to the right of the hostess, Mr. B. to

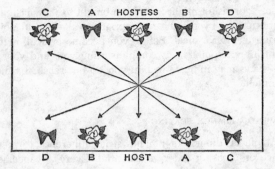

her left. Reverse the placement of the ladies by seating Mrs. B. to the host's right and Mrs. A. to his left.

If seating problems increase with a larger guest list, consider the merits of two tables. The hostess can preside over one and the host over the other. In this arrangement, customarily husbands and wives will not be seated at the same table.

At larger dinners, diplomats and the military often have a seating plan visible to guests as they arrive. This eases seat-finding and gives advance notice of dinner partners.

Unless all present are close friends, place cards should read, "Mrs. Lastname," or "Mr. Lastname," or "General Lastname." Don't use some first names and other guests' last names.

I attended a dinner where most of the guests had not met before. The thoughtful hostess made things easier by writing the names on both sides of the stand-up place cards. This enabled guests to reidentify those across the table. At least it helped those with good eyesight!

AT THE TABLE

Except at formal affairs when the men escort the ladies to dinner, the hostess leads the ladies, the men follow.

During dinner the hostess can help guide conversation toward general subjects. If a guest's comments verge on a subject that might imply criticism of the visitor's country, his associates or official policy, the hostess or the host should lead into safer conversational territory.

SMOKING AT THE TABLE

Official guests normally will not smoke unless the hostess takes the initiative and suggests that her guests may smoke if they wish. In that case ash trays should be on the table.

TOASTING

As at any pleasant home dinner, the host may toast his guests. Flatter your visitor by mentioning him, whether or not he is the official guest of honor. Toasts can appropriately be made at any time. Often the host offers the first toast and others follow at will. A closing toast responding to, and thanking, the host and hostess is sometimes given by one of the guests, usually the guest of honor. This is a matter of strict protocol in some countries, but not in the United States.

DOING ONE'S HOMEWORK

A visitor usually knows more about our country than we know about his. Unfortunately, he might interpret our lack of knowledge as lack of regard or interest. Therefore, a considerate hostess, and a guest, too, if she has been forewarned, will try to learn about a visitor's country in advance. It isn't hard to find out something of its geographical location, type of government and other pertinent or unusual facts.

This homework will fortify you to ask interested and intelligent questions, and also alert you as to which subjects to avoid.

Subjects of conversation should be relatively unrestricted, but it is unfair to ask a guest for "off-the-record" remarks or to comment on sensitive subjects. The occasion is a dinner party, not an interview on "Meet the Press."

The object of your research is to create pleasant conversation in which the guest plays the major role—not a lecture platform for yourself.

AFTERMATH

A guest almost invariably writes or telephones his thanks. At times, in formal diplomatic circles, an engraved visiting card is left at the host's home after the party. If one is left at yours, you will understand it means "Thank you."

29. HOUSEGUESTS ARE COMING!

Those words, "Houseguests are coming!" are a prelude to a happy and busy time. Months or even years might have intervened, still, as soon as we are together again, we pick up as though from yesterday's conversation.

Getting ready for houseguests will mean preparations, and perhaps some reorganizing, but the anticipation of seeing close friends keeps it all from being a chore.

No two homes have identical facilities, or are run the same, but everyone can consider the following suggestions and reminders:

1. Remember jet lags.

    Flying from west to east presents little problem the first day. However, don't schedule a dinner party for west-bound travelers the first evening. By the dinner hour, their built-in clocks will scream bedtime.

    Transoceanic flights create even more severe time lags.

2. You may invite for a specified length of time. Planning will be easier if you know exactly how long guests are staying.

3. Give houseguests both privacy and freedom to do what they want—rest, read, walk or sit in the sun.

    Don't schedule every moment; however, it is your town, and you know what it has to offer. Make suggestions and then decide together what to do and see.

4. Before retiring, settle plans for morning—breakfast together or each on his own (with a kitchen-orientation tour).

    No coffee-holic should have to wait. Set up the coffee pot at night, and let the first one up plug it in.

5. If you are used to running your home informally, everyone will be more comfortable if you don't strain to suddenly change your style.

6. Spend a night in the guests' quarters, or give the rooms an extremely critical eye. Check:

   —Reading and make-up lights

   —Assorted short reading matter

   —Pen, pencil, note paper

   —Check bedding carefully to see if there are enough blankets, and if they need cleaning or rebinding.

   —Extra pillows for reading in bed

   —Clothes hangers, including the special kind for skirts and trousers

   —Supply the bathroom carefully. In addition to the essentials, think about the conveniences guests might like: scissors, cleansing tissues, bath oil, lotions, hair spray, nail file.

7. Make the guest room more beautiful with a bouquet of flowers or a plant, and more comfortable with a pitcher or thermos jug of drinking water.

8. When giving a party for houseguests, give them a guest list and briefing beforehand.

9. Before asking other hostesses if you may bring your houseguests to a party, read page 11.

10. Feel free to keep your own important appointments or do household errands. Your guests will understand.

11. If your guests have other friends who live in the area, assure them they are free to make engagements without including you.

12. Unless you run a hotel-style establishment, let guests make their own beds.

13. If help assisted in the house, guests will want to leave them a tip. I would rather pay a bonus than have guests tip, but regrettably tipping is customary and expected. Some guests send a personal gift to regular help instead of tipping.

14. When I have houseguests, I begrudge every moment I have to spend in the kitchen. One shopping bout and a few hours of concentrated cooking can take care of several days' meals. You might inquire about possible special diets, so you can buy accordingly.

15. Tell your friends what type of clothes they will need, both for the weather and the activities you have planned.

OUR CHILDREN'S HOUSEGUESTS

Our children have always had "carte blanche" privileges to bring their friends home. We've loved it as much, or more, than they.

Almost as soon as a child starts school, he discovers the special treat of bringing a close friend home for the night. Next come the slumber parties—a misnomer for sure. When our children brought friends home from high school and college, hospitality was not limited by the number of available beds. The weekend that eleven young men arrived, they tossed coins, then we meted out the sleeping space in this order: beds, sofas, garden chaise longues and Japanese-inn-style on the floor.

For their daytime foraging, we stocked the kitchen with an enormous supply of eggs, bacon, sandwich makings, hamburgers, hot dogs, buns, fruit, raw salad vegetables, and cookies.

They neither expected nor wanted to be waited on. We were impressed by how well they kept the kitchen cleaned, and made their beds—or floor space! Best of all, each young man wrote an enthusiastic letter of thanks for a wonderful time.

EASY MENU IDEAS FOR A LONG WEEKEND WITH HOUSEGUESTS

Good meals convey such a feeling of warmth and hospitality they are worth advance effort. Go on a cooking spree before guests arrive. If you have freezer space, your spree can take place weeks ahead; if not, cook the day before. Food to be frozen should be handled with care. Quick-cool by plunging your pan or bowl into cold water, and freeze promptly. Stars indicate do-ahead dishes:

Dinners:

—A roast, turkey or ham the evening guests arrive will also take care of lunch sandwiches and children's between-meal nibbles.

—*Veal scallopini is better when made ahead and reheated. Serve with noodles and a frozen or baked vegetable.

—*Lamb or beef casserole, including rice and vegetable, or a boned-chicken-breast casserole with one of many delicious sauces.

—If you have a slow cooker, start a stew before going off for a day's jaunt.

—*If you have a microwave oven, you already know its incredible speed.

—Make shish kabobs and let them marinate until time to barbecue or broil.

Vegetables:

—*Make casseroles of spinach with cheese sauce, squash, tomatoes, artichokes, or string beans with French-fried onion rings or almonds, or use quick-cooking fresh or frozen vegetables. Most vegetables steam by the time one pours water and lights candles.

—*Rice can be cooked ahead, tossed with artichoke hearts, uncooked peas, mushrooms or grated carrots and celery, ready to reheat.

First Courses:
—*Soups, either hot or cold, can be cooked ahead or assembled from cans.

—*Boil eggs to have on hand for salads, sandwiches or hors d'oeuvres.

—*Make molded salad or marinated vegetables.

Desserts:
—*Frozen or refrigerator dessert

—*Cake

—*Crêpes, made ahead and frozen. Add sauce and flame.

Lunches:
—Soups, sandwiches and salads are all easy. Cheese soufflé to go from freezer to oven (page 63).

Breakfasts:
—Breakfasts are usually short-order cooking. If your houseguests are hearty eaters, have plenty of fruit, eggs, breakfast pastry, bacon, sausages or ham.

Miscellaneous:
—Seasoned cheese keeps beautifully, and other appetizers freeze well.

If your houseguests include children, you might want to plan some "Adults Only" meals, with a duplicate menu or something simpler served separately to the children. The children enjoy being alone and sharing their secrets.

Chances are you will go out to at least one lunch or dinner. Maybe with all these advance preparations to choose from, you will have to invite your guests to extend their visit.

30. ENTERTAINING AT A CLUB, HOTEL OR RESTAURANT

Entertaining at home is very personal and always a compliment to your guests. However, at times when home entertaining is inconvenient or impossible, a club or restaurant can come to your rescue.

To assume your responsibilities are over once you've made reservations is a mistake; one should plan as thoughtfully as if entertaining at home.

AT YOUR CLUB

You are already familiar with your club's facilities and specialities and have fewer details to check. Taking a couple or two to dinner at the club takes no more effort than dialing the telephone for reservations. Guests order from the menu or select from a buffet.

For a large arranged dinner, it is still necessary to discuss:

—Drinks and appetizers

—Detailed menu

—Wine

—Flowers or other decorations

—Location of your table, or a separate room

—The serving hour

—The decision as to extra help—such as a cloakroom attendant, parking attendants or an employee to direct guests to your party

When going out of town, check to see if your club has reciprocal privileges with clubs in other cities. If you've been entertained, this is a pleasant way to pay back friends the evening before you leave.

Without having a club to turn to, a friend can sometimes arrange a guest card to his club. As parents of the groom, you will be particularly thankful for the use of a club for the rehearsal dinner.

AT A HOTEL OR RESTAURANT

1. For spur-of-the-moment entertaining, select a restaurant you enjoy or one with a fine reputation.

2. Dinner need not be ordered in advance if the group is small. But remember that guests might guide themselves by the right-hand column and hesitate to order an expensive item unless the host or hostess suggests and encourages. Not "Will you have dessert?" but "What shall we have for dessert?"

   For four or six people, the host can sum up and give the complete order to the captain or waiter. This is an accepted practice in restaurants where service is excellent. Other times, the waiter will take orders in rotation around the table to facilitate bringing each person his order without further questioning or confusion.

3. At a hotel, hosts sometimes register for the night, then serve drinks and appetizers in their room before going to the dining room.

For More Than Eight
1. It is advisable to order in advance for more than eight. Service and food will be better if the chef has had time to give your order his personal attention.

2. When making arrangements, ask whomever is in charge—the manager, maître d'hotel, captain or catering department—for suggestions and recommendations. A personal trial run can turn into a pleasant tasting

party if you order one dish and your husband another for comparisons.

3. If you arrange by telephone (or by letter for out of town entertaining), you can ask the establishment to submit:

   —Several menus from which to choose

   —Wine list. Do you want both white and red?

   —Prices

and specify:

   —Private dining room or desired location of table

   —For a large group, arrangement of tables, "U," "T," or smaller tables

PAYING THE BILL

At your club, arrange to sign the chit in advance or afterward.

At a restaurant, to avoid being presented with the bill in front of guests, you may arrange to:

—Quietly excuse yourself and take care of the bill while guests are drinking coffee.

—Give the maître d'hotel your credit card when you arrive and sign it away from the table.

—Arrange a charge account ahead of time, and have the bill mailed.

—A woman entertaining in a restaurant can handle the bill in one of the ways mentioned, or she can give the money ahead of time to a man guest and ask him to take care of the bill.

TIPPING

—Most clubs do not permit tipping but add a service charge to the bill.

—At your request, a hotel or restaurant will add an agreed-upon percentage to your bill for tips (15 per cent to 20 per cent is customary as of this writing). This arrangement smooths tipping, especially for those who have difficulties with percentages or mental arithmetic.

—Catering departments do not expect tips for making arrangements; arranging is their business.

—One does not tip a restaurant owner.

—Don't forget the wine steward and captain as well as your waiter.

—If a man goes to the same restaurant regularly, he will probably give the maître d' a Christmas remembrance. If this is a one-time visit, he may tip at the time if he requests special services.

REMINDERS

1. Be certain to arrive well ahead of time to arrange seating. Bring place cards already filled out. Check the tables and flowers, and be ready to greet guests.

2. Don't keep prompt arrivals huddled in the foyer. Ask the maître d'hotel to seat you and show latecomers to your table.

3. A host may, if he wishes, tip the cloakroom attendant for checking *all* the coats.

4. Seating charts are a help at large club or restaurant parties held in a private room (page 31).

A LARGE AFFAIR

The catering department is used to handling large functions and will carry out all your wishes. Be explicit. Caterers can engage music and order floral decorations unless you wish to handle them yourself.

You are freed of many details when entertaining away from home. Use some of that reserved energy to see that the party expresses your ideas. Don't sit back and let "them" give the party for you.

We attended a thoughtfully planned dinner at a club. A lovely centerpiece of mixed flowers held lighted candles. After dinner the hostess gathered the ladies' place cards and used them for a drawing. The guest whose card was drawn was given the centerpiece to take home.

A marvelous idea, I thought—especially when I was the winner!

31. THE CAN'T- OR WON'T-EAT DILEMMA

Rarely does a hostess escape at least one disheartening experience of preparing a delicious meal, only to discover, too late, that a guest cannot, or will not, eat it.

A hostess sympathizes with guests on restricted diets, but is less understanding of whims and fads. Regardless of her feelings, she hopes to avoid most diet problems by planning thoughtfully or coping with them tactfully should they occur.

Having been oriented early in life to the school of you-don't-have-to-like-it, you-just-have-to-eat-it, I was mentally unprepared for my finicky friend at my first luncheon party as a bride.

During lunch it developed that she didn't like cheese (there went my sky-high soufflé). She didn't like tomatoes (my tomato aspic). She hated cucumbers (a new recipe for Danish pickled cucumbers). As I recall, even the dessert was on her personal black list.

My trauma increased as each dish was rejected with a polite, "No, thank you, I'm really not hungry." Not hungry! "By now she has to be starved," I thought. In reverse ratio, her list of won't-eat items grew longer as my meager list of suggested substitutions shrank, until suddenly we both burst out laughing. I finally produced two hard-boiled eggs and a grapefruit to initiate the diet she insisted she'd been postponing.

We both survived, but I still think a guest is kinder to make a pretense of eating. One needn't overdo it as my husband once did. I remember watching him eat brussels sprouts—his most disliked vegetable. The hostess commented that she was delighted he liked them because not everyone did. "They're delicious," he said. Then, spurred on by her pleased look, he added untruthfully, "My favorite!"

That was all the encouragement the hostess needed. Ever since, she *always* serves us brussels sprouts, and each time she remarks proudly to my husband, "I remembered how much you loved them and ordered them especially for you."

SAFE PLANNING

1. Garlic-haters abound. If you must use it, do so with a light touch. Offer one salad dressing or one toasted bread with garlic, and one without.

2. Serve cucumbers in a separate bowl instead of mixing them in a salad.

3. If you are considering shellfish as a main course, find out if guests can eat it. If it is merely an appetizer, don't worry—a guest can pass it by if he wishes.

4. When serving dessert sauce, pass two bowls—chocolate and another choice. Chocolate-lovers will appreciate the gesture.

5. Don't hesitate to serve hot chocolate fondue.* It is composed of two parts, and dieters can enjoy the non-chocolate half.

6. Don't serve exotic foods without checking first. Many people dislike escargots, raw fish, brains and other innards, or maybe just the names or connotations make them squeamish. If guests would normally not eat one of these foods, but do so because it is disguised by a hearty sauce, they feel tricked and resentful.

   Game, an epicure's delight to many, is not everyone's dish. If you haven't checked on it, you had better prepare an alternate such as chicken.

7. Don't encourage a guest to break her reducing diet "just this once." Offer fruit in place of a rich dessert. If she has hunger pangs when she leaves the table, she

will know she is on her way toward losing another pound.

So far, we have been more concerned with the *won't*-eaters, now let us look into the more serious problem of those who *cannot* eat specific foods.

In general, it is the guest's responsibility to tell his hostess if he is on a special diet; it is the hostess' responsibility to make her guest feel comfortable—no matter what!

If a guest cannot eat certain foods, you, as hostess, can respond in one of several ways:

1. Assure the guest you are happy to add some acceptable selections to the menu.

2. Invite the guest to drop in before or after dinner.

3. Make the guest feel comfortable about bringing his own food in individual baking dishes ready to reheat.

4. Pretend not to notice if the guest takes only token servings; he probably ate at home.

Note: All churches will gladly clear up your questions about possible diet restrictions. Feel free to call.

When a guest forewarns you (as he should), there is no problem; when you are taken by surprise, what can you do?

You can turn to your emergency shelf (page 44). Offer a substitute, but don't insist. Calmness and flexibility in this situation will mark you as a gracious hostess.

Try to use good judgment when planning menus, but nothing beats a little luck.

RECIPE

TWO-WAY CHOCOLATE FONDUE

Those who can't, or won't, eat chocolate will still have a satisfying dessert.

½ cup (120 ml.) whipping cream, half and half, or evap-
    orated milk
6 ounces (168 gms.) semisweet chocolate bits or candy bar
2 or more tablespoons (30 ml.) kirsch, rum or brandy
Dash of cinnamon
(Variations: Add instant coffee, vanilla or brown sugar)

Ahead of time:
    Combine everything in the top of a double boiler. Stir and
heat until smooth. Keep over warm water until serving time.
    On a large plate, arrange an assortment of bite-sized apples,
bananas, strawberries, pineapple, mandarin oranges, lady fingers, pound or angel food cake, marshmallows.

At serving time:
    Transfer fondue to a chafing dish or fondue pot and place it,
along with the fruit and cake assortment, in the center of the
table within reach of all.
    Give each guest a plate and fondue fork; he may dip into the
chocolate or not as he wishes.

32. WINE

With the growing popularity of wine—for drinking, or collecting as an investment—the subject is worth more than a passing mention when thinking about entertaining.

Many excellent books are devoted entirely to wines, and provide in-depth information for those who want to delve into the subject. Additional information can be gleaned from others who are knowledgeable, including the manager of your bottle shop.

But wine is not sold exclusively at bottle shops. Frequently a jug or bottle of wine is picked up along with the day's groceries at the supermarket where there is seldom anyone to advise. Following are a few considerations:

1. Before buying a new type of wine for a party, have a private tasting at home.

2. Don't judge a wine solely by its cost. Rely on your own taste, and buy only what appeals to you.

3. Imported versus domestic?

    —To serve imported wine was once considered a status symbol. Now many people have discovered domestic wines they are pleased to serve.

    —In most cases there is very little difference in price.

4. "Wine" is not limited to red and white in all its variations. Dubonnet, sherry, port and vermouth are also considered wines.

INSTEAD OF COCKTAILS

As wine becomes increasingly popular, it is important to have a good supply on hand at cocktail parties (page

90, item 2). However, a party at which nothing but wine is served is most pleasant and not at all unusual.

1. Call it an "Open House," instead of a cocktail party.

2. If expense is a consideration, the cost of wine is substantially less than hard liquor.

3. Serve both red and white wine, but count on a lopsided ratio—about 75 per cent white to 25 per cent red wine consumed.

    This preference may be attributed to the fact that, at cocktail time, people enjoy something cold. A glass of well-chilled white wine is more refreshing than room-temperature red wine.

4. Use good-sized wine glasses; an all-purpose eight-ounce glass is ideal.

5. When serving a large number of people, it is more attractive and convenient to pour wine from large decanters instead of bottles or jugs.

AT DINNER

Here is a chance to review some facts and discard some fantasies about wine:

1. People no longer feel bound by the maxim of white wine with fish and poultry, red wine with red meat. Serve what pleases you, or what you think your guests will enjoy, or give them a choice.

2. White wines are best chilled, but they needn't be kept in the refrigerator for hours; an hour is long enough. Red wines are best served at room temperature.

3. The same wine may be served from first course through dessert. If you are giving a formal dinner, or just feel adventurous, serve an appropriate wine with each course:

    —Light wine with soup or salad

—Robust red wine with the main course

—Champagne or fruity white wine with dessert

There are many possibilities and combinations. Don't hesitate to get advice from a connoisseur or an authoritative wine book.

4. The instruction to let wine "breathe" has now been exposed as a myth. If the wine is not good before uncorking, no amount of breathing will help. However, if you find it more convenient to open the wine early, go ahead; it won't be harmed.

5. If you have an especially fine old bottle, you might do well to decant it, so that sediment will not accidentally be poured into a guest's glass.

6. Even though turning a wine glass upside down is not the proper way to say, "No, thank you," understand that your guest means to be considerate and not waste your wine.

7. "Wine snob" is the unflattering name given one who tries to impress. Swishing wine in the mouth is really not necessary to enjoyment, nor attractive to see.

8. Did you know that if you rub the rim of an opened bottle of wine with waxed paper, there will be no drips? Amazing! You needn't wrap the bottle in a towel, unless you want to conceal the label.

COOKING WITH WINE

Wines used in cooking give an illusive, marvelous flavor —in sauces, stews, fish dishes, even salad dressings. The alcoholic content burns off during the cooking, but the flavor remains.

The better the quality of wine, the better the flavor. If you aren't ready to open a bottle of white wine at the moment you need it for cooking, add dry vermouth instead. Some cooks prefer its flavor and use it by choice.

Books featuring cooking with wine are available in bookstores, cooking-ware shops and libraries. From them one learns how to turn plain, ordinary food into something quite special.

WINE-TASTING PARTY

If you have ever attended a wine-tasting party, you know it can be both fun and enlightening.

Unless you are an expert, get advice from the manager of your bottle shop. He can help you select a good tasting assortment of imported and domestic wines in various price ranges—but not so many it becomes confusing.

1. Cover the labels and number each bottle. Keep a record nearby with the pertinent information.

2. Give each guest a score card to fill in the following answers about each wine:
   a. Identify its type, such as chablis, chenin blanc, burgundy, beaujolais or others.
   b. Imported or domestic.
   c. Rate in descending order of personal preference.
   d. Rate from most to least expensive.

3. Between tastings serve cubes of bread or bland crackers to remove the taste of the old wine before sampling the new.

4. When everyone has filled out his card, collect and score them to find the winner.

5. A suitable prize for the winner might be a bottle of wine, or something else to do with wine, such as a wine coaster, a corkscrew, or a book about wines.

WINE STORAGE

A wine cellar is a luxury for the average person, and not a necessity except to serious collectors. Those who plan to store for years can study and consult experts. Even then, there are differences of opinion over a degree or two of temperature.

Wine should be kept in a cool, dry place. A kitchen cupboard is not recommended because of the heat generated by one's regular appliances. A basement, a garage or storage room is usually satisfactory, or even a shelf in a linen or clothes closet.

Store the bottles on their sides to keep the corks moist. Once a cork dries out, it contracts and air gets into the bottle—to the detriment of the wine.

RECIPES

WINE COOLER

Fill a tall glass with equal parts of red wine and 7-Up, lots of ice, and a slice of lemon. Or substitute club soda for the 7-Up. Bulk wines are suitable for this refreshing drink.

CHAMPAGNE AND ORANGE JUICE

Combine equal parts of champagne and orange juice in ice-filled glasses. Delicious before brunch.

APPETIZER CHEESE

Mix a little sherry or brandy with sharp Cheddar cheese to make a delicious spread on crackers.

33. TIME-SAVERS AND REMINDERS

There is so much a hostess has to do, and wants to do, that she should take advantage of every possible short cut. I have found a few time-savers and do-aheads which I pass along to you.

TIME-SAVERS

1. Are your habits hindering your work? For years, I kept the coffee pot at one end of the kitchen and the toaster at the other. I shudder to think how many unnecessary steps a pedometer would have registered.

2. Efficient cooks recommend lining up every ingredient a recipe calls for, down to the last seasoning before starting to combine and mix. As you use each item, place it to one side. Not only does this method save backtracking steps, but it also serves as a double check that nothing was omitted.

3. When you empty the dishwasher, instead of putting everything away, think ahead. Place whatever you will need for the next meal on a tray, ready to carry to the dining room.

4. If you have huge quantities of lettuce to prepare for tossed salad, swish it in the sink and then into a nylon-mesh laundry bag. Put in the washing machine and spin out the excess water in a few seconds.

5. If you feel you are wasting time on the telephone, buy a shoulder-rest gadget. Your hands will be free to fix your nails or sew. A friend completed twin bedspreads consisting of over four thousand little circles on "wasted time."

You might also use telephone time to lie on the floor and do leg exercises.

6. It takes less time to remove a place setting or two than to add them later. If you are uncertain as to how many guests are coming, set the table for the maximum number.

7. Tuck stamped, addressed envelopes or post cards into your handbag and write notes in otherwise-wasted moments in waiting rooms or under the dryer. Warning: Seal each letter immediately to avoid inadvertently switching letters and envelopes—an embarrassing mistake I once made.

8. My biggest time-saver concerns dressing. I used to dress first for morning chores then change later to going-out clothes. Now I dress completely for whatever I will do later—except to slip into my dress. Savings: thirty minutes or more.

9. A microwave oven saves both cooking and pot-washing time.

TIPS

10. For note-making to yourself or family members: Screw a rectangle of clear plastic to the kitchen wall. Use a broad-tipped marker with washable ink.

11. Devise your own morale-builders or games to make household tasks more pleasant. One friend saves her old evening clothes to wear for grubby jobs; she says they brainwash her into believing she is doing something glamorous.

Another friend sets her timer for short periods of work to be followed by rewards—perhaps eating a piece of candy, reading an article, chatting on the phone, or taking a short walk.

12. While concentrating on your far-away BIG project, don't forget your family has to eat in the meantime.

13. When you telephone a friend, don't launch into a long account without asking first if she is busy. If someone calls you at an inconvenient time, feel free to explain, and ask when you can return the call.

14. "Please Come In" are the words a friend needle-worked into a beautiful and useful sign to hang on the doorknob. It relieves one person from answering-the-door duty for large parties or meetings, while still conveying a feeling of welcome.

15. A coat rack is useful at other than party times. Bring it out for closet-cleaning days, and before packing for a trip. When everything you contemplate squeezing into your suitcase hangs before your eyes, you can see how much is non-essential, or would call for different sets of accessories. When traveling, too many clothes are a nuisance.

    An inexpensive coat rack, which comes apart for storage, can be constructed from galvanized pipe and screw-on elbow joints. Rubber-tip the feet to prevent scratching the floor or damaging the rug.

16. When serving curry or mustard sauce, use your bleachable white napkins.

17. When serving a lap buffet, plan your menu so a possible spill won't turn into a catastrophe; avoid beet soup, raspberry sauce or other stainers.

18. Should you tell a friend that her lipstick is smeared or her slip shows? Yes, but only *if* she can remedy it.

19. When entertaining, stay with a recipe you are used to, instead of the one a friend swears won't fail. Your oven might be a few degrees off from hers—just enough to prove it *can* fail.

20. With the expense of paper goods, why not make a one-time investment in dozens of small permanent-press napkins—enough for any large party.

21. If you have two ovens, be sure to put the food in the heated one. Obvious? It is to me now, after putting a roast in the wrong oven. We settled for scrambled eggs that evening instead of another two-hour wait.

22. If you are busy with several tasks at once, carry a timer around with you. Set it to remind yourself when to turn off the sprinklers, make a phone call, or check the oven.

23. Now and then take a few minutes to relax completely. Breathe deeply; stretch; lie on the floor and do a shoulder stand for three to five minutes. Those few minutes will be as renewing as a nap.

24. If a guest stays overtime, take heart. He can't stay forever. Start talking about a boring subject such as your next day's list of chores.

DO-AHEADS

25. Cut rounds and other shapes of bread for tea sandwiches or appetizers weeks ahead. Butter and spread them on a cookie sheet and freeze, then store in plastic bags. If you don't freeze them first, the butter will glue them together.

26. Six trays of made-ahead tea sandwiches or hors d'oeuvres—one tray to a shelf—would use up all the shelves in our refrigerator. This problem of space inspired our homemade invention—stackable trays, limited only by the distance between shelves. Six trays stack in about 7½ inches of space.

    Buy cookie sheets to fit your refrigerator. Each end must have a flange with a hole. Make separators out of blocks of wood about one-inch thick. Each block has a hole in one side and a dowel in the other, except for the two base blocks which have two pegs. See the diagram below.

    Place all the tidbits that will need heating on the same cookie sheet, ready to go straight from refrigerator to oven.

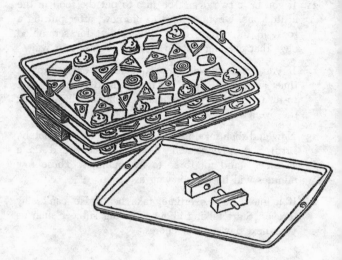

27. If you love bacon, but not greasy broilers or pans, cook a pound or two at one time. Drain the grease and store bacon in plastic bags for a week in the refrigerator—much longer in the freezer. Bacon is instantly available to crumble on sandwiches, salads, hors d'oeuvres and vegetables, or to reheat briefly for breakfasts.

28. Individual salads or salad bowls stay crisp for hours if wrapped in airtight plastic. To keep avocado bright, place its seed in the salad bowl.

29. You needn't wait until the last minute to unmold individual salads. Turn them onto a cookie sheet hours ahead and give them time to reharden if you overdid the warm water. Later, slip them onto the arranged salad plates with a wide spatula.

30. Freeze individual mounds of whipped cream on a cookie sheet, then store in freezer bags. To use, place on desserts to thaw about twenty minutes before serving.

Make pesta sauce when fresh basil is available. Freeze in amounts for single dinners in paper baking cups.

EMERGENCIES

31. Don't apologize if your Grand Marnier soufflé doesn't rise; serve it in dessert glasses and call it Grand Marnier pudding.

32. If something goes wrong, make light of it. Everyone has made mistakes or had disappointments, so they will understand.

    The help I'd engaged for a dinner party failed to show up. A tragedy? No, just some last-minute rearranging and lots of fun. Even with all the kitchen volunteers, dinner was frightfully late, so late that our guests filed through the kitchen, plates in hand, to be served out of the cooking utensils—called "making the best of it."

33. We once arrived for a party—one week early. The hosts welcomed us cordially and insisted we stay. The four of us ate delicious meat loaf sandwiches in front of the fire and then played bridge. I hope, if someone comes to our home on the wrong night, I will be equally hospitable.

    We returned for the scheduled party the next week, and although everything was beautifully planned, it was no more fun than our intimate evening.

34. If a guest should happen to break your most treasured possession, remember that saving "things" is nothing compared to saving feelings.

    A few minutes saved here and a few minutes saved there add up to quite a bit of time. What one does with that extra, found time is up to her. She is not obligated to spend it in another top-speed project. It is hers to relish and *enjoy.*

34. CHECK LIST FOR PARTY EQUIPMENT

Party equipment lists are generally long, and everything on them sounds intriguing. However, I am inclined to treat the lists merely as suggestions for each hostess to evaluate, then establish her own priorities.

To one hostess, a thirty-two-cup coffee maker is top priority for club meetings and other large groups she entertains, while to another who entertains only at small dinners, an oversized coffee pot would do nothing but clutter her kitchen. The same premise holds true for every piece of equipment: soup tureens and fondue pots are marvelous—for those who serve soups and fondues.

It might take a lifetime plus a reincarnation or two to amass all you think you need; however, this current life span should suffice for what you really need for *your* way of entertaining. Borrow or rent in the meantime, then set about acquiring each item, one by one, in the order of its importance to you.

The following list does not mean "buy," it means "think about."

In the Living Room
  —Card tables and covers, and bridge-size tablecloths

  —Ash trays and coasters

  —Suitable vases and planters

  —Extra chairs

  —A nest of tables or TV tables

  —Assortment of games, if this suits your style

In the Dining Room
  —Linens, tablecloths, place mats, napkins

—China, whether all one pattern or of compatible designs

—Crystal: water, wine, cocktail, and dessert

—Wine coaster. A silver or glass plate can substitute

—Silver, flatware and serving dishes. If you advertise your needs, relatives sometimes enjoy adding piece by piece.

—Sectioned vegetable dish

—Candlesticks

—Serving cart

—Centerpiece for arranging flowers

—Place cards

On the Buffet Table
   —Casseroles

—Fondue pots

—Chafing dishes

—Large platters and servers

—Hot trays, large enough to be practical
   Hot trays are more than party equipment. Mine is next to the stove where I use it daily. I always had trouble getting everything to finish cooking at the same time; now, as each dish is ready, I transfer it to the hot tray where it can wait for us. I also use it to heat dinner plates.

—Soup tureen. Choose from electric, thermos-type, porcelain or earthenware. This is a versatile server which one can use occasionally as a centerpiece.

For the Bar
   —An ice bucket, and perhaps an extra large one, too.

Your camping ice chest will take care of patio parties or other informal occasions.

—All-purpose glasses, plus wines and liqueurs should do for a while.

Stocking the bar is covered in the chapter on *Cocktail Parties,* page 89.

In the Kitchen
—Large cooking pots—if you entertain large numbers

—Party-sized coffee maker

—Slow or fast cooker, Crockpot or microwave oven— whichever is your speed.

—Toaster-oven or rotisserie-broiler

In General
—Coat rack and extra hangers

—Finger-tip towels

—Umbrella stand and rainy-weather doormat

Specific Needs for a Specific Party
Perhaps you should pretend you are a guest walking in the front door. From hanging your coat to sitting by a table with ash tray and coaster, you can imagine yourself doing all the things your guests will do, and in this way anticipate all their needs.

Whether it is stocking the bar or arranging the buffet dishes in logical order, pretending you are a guest in this instance is not only fun—it is useful. You are the hostess checking her check list!

35. HOST TODAY, GUEST TOMORROW

The words "host" and "guest" have entirely different meanings; however, in Latin, "hospes" is the single word which means *both* host and guest—an enlightening and appealing definition. It should then follow that a good hostess will also be a good guest.

Max Beerbohm wrote an enchanting essay on the subject of hosts and guests, the essence being that the same person cannot be a success as both—that hosts give, guests receive.

Despite the charm of his essay, I am convinced that a host also receives and a guest gives—that they are indeed one and the same, as in "hospes."

REMINDERS FOR GUESTS

Invitations

1. A hostess, knowing how important prompt responses are to her plans, will respond promptly forevermore—even to answering invitations without R.S.V.P.'s.

2. Ward McAllister made this tongue-in-cheek statement in the 1890s: "A dinner party invitation, once accepted, is a sacred obligation. If you die before the dinner takes place, your executor must attend."

3. It is thoughtless to talk about invitations or parties one has attended in front of anyone who was not invited.

4. Invitations sometimes include a telephone number for responses—a number no one stays home to answer. After an attempt or two, or simply if more convenient, respond by mail.

At Dinners or Other Meals

5. A guest who is normally a slow eater should try to speed up and keep pace with the other guests. He knows his hostess is slowing down because of him.

6. In a restaurant if dinner has been preordered, a guest knows not to ask for substitutions or additions. When ordering from a menu, no one but the host should straighten out the orders or summarize them for the waiter.

   If one wonders how to order, remember that telling one's husband, host, escort or dinner partner and letting him relay the order has long been customary etiquette. Those women who still prefer having men open doors and hold their chairs will find it natural to follow this procedure.

7. If one doesn't care for wine, he should take some and let it stand in his glass. This is less conspicuous than turning the glass upside down.

8. Someone has to sit next to the dull gentleman. If you are chosen, consider it a compliment that the hostess knew you would be gracious.

At a Party

9. As you enter a room, stand still, take a deep breath and look around. Don't charge in only to find yourself in a group of strangers who are in the middle of a conversation.

10. You know a hostess cannot be every place at once, so don't wait to be rescued from a corner. Introduce yourself, and if you see someone else in need of rescue, draw him into your group's conversation.

11. Co-operate with your hostess' plans for games, conversation, seating, timing—anything.

12. When you go to a swimming party, take your own towel, and remember that sun-tan oils are harmful to pools and their equipment.

As a Houseguest

13. Help your hostess without being asked; however, tread lightly in the cooking department. Some women consider that their personal domain. "The Queen was in the kitchen. . . ."

14. Even with help in the house make your own bed, unless the hostess asks you not to. Before leaving, ask for sheets to make the beds for the next guests.

15. Letters of thanks and "bread-and-butter gifts" are always appreciated, no matter how modest.

16. Don't spring your special diet list on your hostess after you arrive. Unless you are willing to eat everything, warn her beforehand so she can market accordingly.

17. A motor-home or boating guest, who wants to bring some part of a day's or weekend's edibles, should consult the hosts. Surprises might be duplications, or create problems of surplus or storage.

    If spending the night, ask about clothing. Wardrobe space is either limited or non-existent.

18. When you are invited to a weekend house offer to bring your bed linens.

In General

19. You know how important the last few minutes might be to the hosts; don't arrive early.

20. If you suspect dinner might be very late, eat a snack beforehand.

21. In a house of non-smokers, step outside to smoke or ask permission. A thoughtful guest will not use every ash tray.

22. If you spill, rubbing the spot could be ruinous. Immediately tell the hostess so she or a maid can give emergency treatment. Offer to call a carpet cleaner even though most hostesses would not accept.

23. Hostesses know whether or not they want their activities reported in newspapers. Therefore, as a guest you know not to give information about parties you attend —even if the party is for you—without permission from the hostess.

24. Neither overstay nor break up the party by leaving too soon. If you must leave early, explain to the hostess or phone the next day, but try to slip away without the usual round of good-byes.

25. People wonder if, after having thanked at the time, additional thank-yous are necessary. You as hostess know that you appreciate a gracious telephone call or note of thanks.

26. When it is time to leave, say good-bye and GO!

ENJOY! The check lists and reminders are for one purpose—to release you so you *will* feel like a guest at your own parties.

Happy entertaining!

APPENDIX

COCKTAIL PARTY

	NUMBER OF GUESTS	QUANTITY TO ORDER	AMOUNT USED	NUMBER OF GUESTS	QUANTITY TO ORDER	AMOUNT USED	
SCOTCH							
BOURBON							
GIN							
VODKA							
RUM							
WHITE WINE							
RED WINE							
VERMOUTH							
SHERRY							
DUBONNET							
BEER							
ICE							
CLUB SODA							
TONIC WATER							
COLA							
GINGER ALE							
JUICES							
GLASSES							
LEMONS							
LIMES							
OLIVES							
TOOTH PICKS							
NAPKINS							

ESTIMATE:
1 quart liquor serves 20 drinks @ 1½ ounces — 7 persons approximately
1 fifth liquor serves 18 drinks @ 1½ ounces — 6 persons approximately
1 fifth wine serves 5 drinks @ 5 ounces
1 gallon wine serves 26 drinks @ 5 ounces

CHECK LIST*

NUMBER OF GUESTS	QUANTITY TO ORDER	AMOUNT USED	NUMBER OF GUESTS	QUANTITY TO ORDER	AMOUNT USED

Note: Guests often place their glasses down and order fresh drinks.
To be safe, figure three drinks per person.

* Refer to page 89